SUPERNATURAL POWER *for* DOMINION

SUPERNATURAL POWER *for* DOMINION

LIVING WITH KINGDOM AUTHORITY IN CHRIST

RON CRAYCRAFT

XULON PRESS

Xulon Press
555 Winderley Pl, Suite 225
Maitland, FL 32751
407.339.4217
www.xulonpress.com

© 2024 by Ron Craycraft
Senior Pastor, Author

www.ForecastForLife.org
Forecast For Life CHURCH

www.GoForecast.Teachable.com
Forecast For Life BIBLE INSTITUTE

All rights reserved solely by the author. The author guarantees all contents are original and do not infringe upon the legal rights of any other person or work. No part of this book may be reproduced in any form without the permission of the author.

Due to the changing nature of the Internet, if there are any web addresses, links, or URLs included in this manuscript, these may have been altered and may no longer be accessible. The views and opinions shared in this book belong solely to the author and do not necessarily reflect those of the publisher. The publisher therefore disclaims responsibility for the views or opinions expressed within the work.

Unless otherwise indicated, Scripture quotations taken from the New King James Version (NKJV). Copyright © 1982 by Thomas Nelson, Inc. Used by permission. All rights reserved.

Scripture quotations taken from the King James Version (KJV) – *public domain*.

Scripture quotations taken from the Amplified Bible (AMP). Copyright © 1954, 1958, 1962, 1964, 1965, 1987 by The Lockman Foundation. Used by permission. All rights reserved.

Paperback ISBN-13: 979-8-86850-350-4
Ebook ISBN-13: 979-8-86850-351-1

The *storms of life* will threaten to *rock your world*. However, your *personal forecast* of God's Word will bring hope, healing, faith, love, peace, and victory through Christ Jesus.

DEDICATION

I dedicate this book to my wonderful wife, Pam – my best friend, best prayer partner, my motivator, my love forever, and my number one encourager in life and ministry!

TABLE OF CONTENTS

Introduction. xiii

Chapter 1	God's Gift of Dominion	1
Chapter 2	Jesus Restored Dominion	11
Chapter 3	The Kingdom of Power	19
Chapter 4	Kingdom Benefits Are Here	29
Chapter 5	It is Not a Faith Problem.	39
Chapter 6	Dunamis Power.	47
Chapter 7	Powered By the Spirit	57
Chapter 8	Dominion in Action	65
Chapter 9	Dominion Is Not for Wimps	77
Chapter 10	Dominion and Authority.	85
Chapter 11	Dominion of Kings and Priests.	95
Chapter 12	Called to Conquer.	103
Chapter 13	Your Position of Power	111
Chapter 14	Exousia Power.	117
Chapter 15	Keys of the Kingdom.	127
Chapter 16	Breaking Demonic Strongholds	135
Chapter 17	Dominion From The 3rd Heaven	141
Chapter 18	Dominion Releases God's Power.	145
Chapter 19	Dominion and Anointing	151
Chapter 20	What Dominion Really Means.	159
Chapter 21	The Truth About Dominion	167
Chapter 22	3 Keys to Kingdom Living	177
Chapter 23	How-to Walk-in Miracles.	189
Chapter 24	Your Super Powerful Life	197

Authority is your God-given right, to take 'dominion' over circumstances.

INTRODUCTION

"As an eagle stirs up its nest, hovers over its young, spreading out its wings, taking them up, carrying them on its wings." (**Deut. 32:11**)

Born-again, Spirit-led Christians have been gifted with the power to *dominate* sin, sickness, demons, and fear! In fact, Christians already have the power within to overcome addictions, pride, grief, insecurity, and selfishness.

If this good news is a surprise to you, or if you want to hear more about God's gift of dominion—fasten your spiritual seatbelt, take off your religious hat, and get ready to receive the whole truth about God's plan for mankind.

Thankfully, I have learned that God's will and power is beyond the visible observable universe. God's supernatural blessings are unexplainable by natural laws. If we want to receive His will and power – we must see, hear, and know Him spiritually. God *"has blessed us with every spiritual blessing in the heavenly places in Christ"* (**Eph 1:3**). Now we pray and believe, *"Your will be done on earth as it is in heaven"* (**Matt 6:10**).

Supernatural power for dominion is powerful, controversial, and radical to the casual believer. However, I believe this study will be well worth your attention and could be life changing. It was for me!

Even though this is a deep subject, it will be easy to activate in your life, starting right in your own home, in your business, and in your community. College degrees, attending big healing revival meetings, and having thousands of people praying for you is wonderful, but these things are not required. According to the scriptures, God "*sent His **word** and healed them, And delivered them from their destructions.*" (**Ps. 107:20.**)

Something Was Missing

I have always said that I believe the whole Word of God. I have also believed that praying the Word of God is the answer to every problem. However, when confronted with a big mountain of circumstances—my best prayer seemed to fall short. I did not really believe that I had real supernatural kingdom power, like the scriptures say I do (see **Rom 8:11**).

What was my problem? What was I missing?

I am totally convinced through my intense study of the New Testament scriptures—that God is ***always*** good (see **Jas. 1:17**), and God is love. God ***always*** says yes to all His promises (see **2 Cor. 1:20**). Satan is the one who promotes sickness, disease, accidents, crisis, and trouble. "*The thief does not come except to steal, and to kill, and to destroy.*" (**Jn. 10:10-a.**) Nevertheless, Jesus came "*that they may have life, and that they may have it more abundantly.*" (**Jn. 10:10b.**) *There is a huge difference between the Old Testament and the New Testament—it is the Cross, where we have grace and forgiveness of all sin.

> God's plan was and is to give humanity dominion over the earth.

So, what was it that I did not understand?

I did not have a good *revelation knowledge* of God's plan for mankind. In other words, I did not have the best understanding of the "good news" of the gospel of God's Kingdom that I thought I had!

Now I am realizing that God's plan has never changed since Genesis. God's plan was and is to give humanity dominion over the earth. Moreover, the last Adam, Jesus the Christ, lived and demonstrated that dominion everywhere He went for 3 ½ years.

Introduction

> *"God created man in His own image; in the image of God He created him; male and female He created them. Then God blessed them, and God said to them, "Be fruitful and multiply; fill the earth and subdue it; have dominion."* **Gen 1:26**

> To make the point even clearer, *"The heaven, even the heavens, are the LORD's; But the earth He has given to the children of men."* (**Ps. 115:16** and **Ps. 8:4-6**.)

Many good, church-going Christians are missing a vital ingredient in living the abundant life that Jesus came to give us (see **Jn. 10:10**). Even though you are living, a godly life and you are very spiritual—there is a Bible principle that could unlock the victories that will make you, *"more than a conqueror"* even in times of trouble. (**Rom. 8:37**.)

The New Covenant is Better

Picture yourself in the desert, weary and tired, just like the Israelites on the verge of giving up on finding their promised land. Then imagine God telling you to rise-up and take it (see **Deut. 2:24**). What does a command to rise-up look like in your life? How would things change if you *rise-up* in your health, finances, family, or job, and started fulfilling the purpose God's placed in your heart (see **Ps. 37:4** and **Col. 3:15**)?

To me, *rise-up* reminds me of the golden eagle! When confronted with a powerful storm, the eagle will rise far above the storm—between 10,000 and 20,000 feet above sea level. Believers can also *rise-up* above the powerful spiritual storms that confront them, with "Supernatural Power for Dominion."

Soaring Above Man-Made Traditions

Like an eagle, believers must use their spiritual strength in Christ to overcome argumentative traditions that say miracles have passed away. Miracles are happening every day in the twenty-first century. Every Christian must consider that Jesus is the miracle worker! Then in Hebrews, we know that, *"Jesus Christ is the same yesterday, today, and forever."* (**Heb. 13:8.**)

The Lord Jesus promised that His Holy Spirit would come upon you (see **Acts 1:8**) and fill you with power, divine power in the inner man, supernatural power—God power.

If you have said yes to Jesus as your Lord (see **Rom. 10:9**). Then, receive Jesus as your baptizer with the Holy Spirit and power (see **Matt. 3:11, Lk. 11:13, Acts 2:1-4,** and **Acts 19:2**).

Now you simply need to discover how to access and use this power to bless others.

That is what this book is for and what you are on earth for. Get ready to plug in. Get ready to become a 'kingdom messenger' of Holy Spirit power.

Praying or Taking Dominion

You do not have to choose between prayer and dominion. Believers should be doing both! Unfortunately, most Christians do not know anything about dominion—until now!

From now on, believers will be speaking directly to their bodies, to circumstances, and to mountains of problems in Jesus' mighty name (see **Mk. 11:23**). You will resist the devil and he will flee from you (see **Jas. 4:7**).

Dominion is what will help you to do the same works that Jesus did, (see **Jn. 14:12**). Do you realize that Jesus did not pray (ask) when He healed people? Read the four gospels. Jesus used God-given dominion to speak to wind, storms, trees, demons, and sick people. He said, be still, come out, he healed, and stretch out your withered hand.

Jesus did not ask, He took authority by the gift of dominion to do miracles! Jesus said, *"he who believes in Me, the works that I do he will do also."* (**Jn. 14:12.**)

You can do this. I know you can—from first-hand experience!

"Dominion" is God's original plan to soar above trouble.

Chapter 1
God's Gift of Dominion

"And God said, Let us make man in our image, after our likeness: and let them have dominion." (**Gen. 1:26**)

Genesis shows what the plan of God has always been (see **Gen. 1:26**). God created the Earth, and He put Adam in charge. He created the Earth for His children to enjoy and oversee. Adam's assignment was to take care of everything God created. The Earth still belongs to God, but Adam was the caretaker. In fact, Adam was given God's dominion power over the Earth. In Genesis it says,

"And God said, Let us make man in our image, after our likeness: and let them have dominion over the fish of the sea, and over the fowl of the air, and over the cattle, and over all the earth, and over every creeping thing that creepeth upon the earth. So God created man in his own image, in the image of God created he him; male and female created he them. And God blessed them, and God said unto them, Be fruitful, and multiply, and replenish the earth, and subdue it: and have dominion over the fish of the sea, and over the fowl of the air, and over every living thing that moveth upon the earth." **Gen. 1:26-28**

The Hebrew word for dominion is *râdâh*, and it is pronounced *raw-daw'*. The definition is: *to tread down, that is, subjugate; have dominion—prevail against, reign, rule, and take charge of.*

Notice what God kept saying: "Have dominion." *Dominion* literally means to *tread down*. It can mean to *put under your foot*, or to *hold in place under your foot*, so it means to have absolute *authority*.

Does anybody have a problem with Adam having absolute authority? No, they should not, but some people do. If you are religious at all (I am using that term in a negative sense), you could say, "Well, it could not be absolute dominion because God has absolute dominion."

God does have absolute dominion, but He gave Adam *an area* over which he would have dominion. That is what you must realize. If you understand that, then you also understand what the Bible means when it speaks about the truth of the true sovereignty of God.

True sovereignty does not mean fickle. It does not mean God will do whatever He wants to do, anytime He wants to do it. Sovereignty means that God is all-supreme—no one is even close to being as high as God. Nevertheless, at the same time, He has relegated Himself to operate within 'His own commands' and within the laws that He Himself has set.

In other words, no one is above God, and no one can tell God what to do. Although, God Himself has established spiritual and physical laws that He will abide by. If we know what is good for us, we will abide by His laws too!

Notice He gave man dominion. He gave man absolute authority over this Earth. Psalms mentions this several times.

In the book of Psalms it says,

> "*The heaven, even the heavens, are the LORD'S: but the earth hath he given to the children of men. The heavens belong to God, but the earth He has given to the children of men; the sons of men.*" **Ps. 115:16**

God owns the heavens, but He put the kingdom of the Earth under man's dominion. We know, according to Jesus, that Satan tried to tempt Him. It tells us this in the Gospel of Luke,

> *"And the devil said unto him, All this power will I give thee, and the glory of them: for that is delivered unto me; and to whomsoever I will I give it. If thou therefore wilt worship me, all shall be thine."* **Lk. 4:6-7**

The devil said to him, "I will give you all of this power and the glory of all of this Earthly kingdom if You will just bow Your knee." In effect he said, "Dominion power was delivered to me, and I can give it to whomever I want."

When was power and dominion given to Satan? Dominion was given to him when Adam accepted the temptation in the garden. It was then that he handed the power and the dominion over to the devil. It is a scriptural principle that Adam activated: *"Do you not know that to whom you present yourselves slaves to obey, you are that one's slaves whom you obey."* (**Rom. 6:16**.)

Notice the only power that Satan has been working under is the dominion that God had given to man. Notice that all of that was offered back to Jesus, but Jesus did not take it because He knew that it was a shortcut. He knew He was going to get it anyway. *Dominion* is *absolute authority*.

Jesus was going to take back this dominion—the hard way...the spiritually legal way!

Your Position in Christ

Today, Jesus sits at the right hand of God the Father; and spiritually, we believers have been raised up together to sit with Him (see **Eph 2:4-6**). Jesus is interceding for us; meaning that He is cheering for us to take our place as sons and daughters of God. Unfortunately, instead of viewing things from heaven's perspective, many Christians are still focused on the natural things of this Earth.

Many Christians are so focused on the natural world that they forget Satan is the 'god' of this world and he wants to sway us more and more into his domain. He is *"the prince of the power of the air,"* (**Eph. 2:2**) and a principality that we should be resisting with our authority. Satan's number one weapon is deceit.

Satan deceived Adam and Eve in the Garden. He succeeded in his strategy of tricks to get God's son and daughter to doubt what God has said. In Matthew, he tried the same tactic against Jesus in the wilderness (see **Matt. 4:3**). On the other hand, now Jesus, the last Adam, refused to fall for the trap. Jesus, grounded in the truth of God's Word, would not doubt who He was as the Son of God.

> Believers can rise above trouble just like an eagle rises high up over the storms of life

Satan's tactic is to get believers to doubt God's Word and to question the authority that we have in Christ. When Satan is successful, believers disqualify themselves in their own minds.

God, the Creator of everything, is a spirit (see **Jn. 4:24**). God's words are spirit and life (see **Jn. 6:63**). God is upholding all things by the word of His power (see **Heb. 1:3**). It may not seem right to our natural thinking, but God's *words* are the *seeds of our miracle* (see **Mk. 4:13-20**). God's Word guarantees power to all who will receive, (see **Acts 1:8**).

God's Gifts of Power and Authority

Every believer is an overcomer and is victorious because they have eternal life in Christ (see **Jn. 3:16.**) and because Jesus came to give us abundant life, *in this life* (see **Jn. 10:10**). God's Spirit lives within the believer to provide power to overcome the tribulations of this world (see **Jn. 16:33**). Believers can rise above trouble just like an eagle rises high up over the storms of life (see **Ps. 103:4-5, Is 40:31**).

The Will and purpose of God has always been to give *power to His people*, (see **Gen. 1:26, Ps. 115:16**).

"For everyone who has been born of God overcomes the world. And this is the victory that has overcome the world–our faith." (**1 Jn. 5:4**.) In this passage of scripture, John simply refers to "faith" as our victory. Remember, the faith of the believer is the victory that overcomes.

Jesus cannot be overpowered by darkness (see **Jn. 1:5**.) and He has defeated the powers of this world (see **Jn. 16:33.**). Believers are not to be overcome by evil but overcome evil with good (see **Rom. 12:21**). Believers should be ruling and reigning in life through Christ, (see **Rom. 5:17**).

> Real believers do not just believe the works of Jesus—they 'do' the works of Jesus

Believers should overcome both the evil one (see **1 Jn. 2:13–14.**) and evil spirits (see **1 Jn. 4:4**). Christians are not left weak and defenseless in spiritual battles. On the contrary, Christ already won those battles.

It is Your Responsibility

Dominion and authority for the believer is not a take it or leave it gift. God has *already* made mankind to have dominion in the Earth (see **Gen. 1:26-28** and **Ps. 115:16**). New Covenant believers do not *'just believe.'* Real believers do not just believe the works of Jesus—they *'do'* the works of Jesus (see **Jn. 14:1**)!

Hebrews gives us a clear picture of how believers should be living.

> *"God, who at various times and in various ways spoke in time past to the fathers by the prophets, has in these last days spoken to us by His Son, whom He has appointed heir of all things, through whom also He made the worlds."* **Heb. 1:1**

If you want to experience the deep things of the spirit (authority, dominion, God's healing power, spiritual gifts, miracles, divine health)—**read, listen to, and sing** the things that, reinforce and strengthen your belief in the supernatural power of God (see **Matt. 16:18-19**)!

The truth is that we are not waiting for God to heal—God is waiting on us to receive and activate what He has already provided (see **Eph. 1:3, 1 Pet. 2:24**)!

Jesus gave us His authority and dominion when He said, *"I give you authority…"* (**Lk. 10:19.**) Jesus also gave authority to believers as we read, (see **Lk. 9:1, Matt. 10:8, Ps. 115:16, Mk. 11:23,** and **Mk. 16:17-18.**) All dominion and authority are *delegated* from Jesus to believers!

Dominion Over What?

The answer to what we have dominion over is ultimately over the Earth, and its sin, sickness, demons, and fear. We should take dominion over our health. Take dominion over our thoughts. Take dominion over our words.

A powerful declaration of the gospel by Jesus explains what we should dominate:

> *"The Spirit of the Lord is upon me, because he hath anointed me to preach the gospel to the poor; he hath sent me to heal the brokenhearted, to preach deliverance to the captives, and recovering of sight to the blind, to set at liberty them that are bruised."* **Lk. 4:18**

Therefore, we should dominate at least five situations that have plagued humanity since the fall of man.

Sin, sickness, demons, poverty, and early death—all these proceed from Satan's kingdom of darkness, (see **Jn. 10:10.**).

Manifestations of Dominion

There are three requirements for supernatural manifestation (results). **First**, we ask for a Rhema word from God. Rhema, meaning an anointed spoken word from God, which is hearing a word (see **Rom. 10:17**), while in daily communion with the Lord. **Second**, we need to speak and believe (see **Mk. 11:23**) the Rhema word that we personally heard from the Lord. In other words, we cannot just imitate someone else's teaching or testimony and get results (see **Jn. 14:21**). **Third**, we need to limit the amount of unbelief that tries to invade our lives on a daily basis (see **Matt. 17:18-21**).

Demonstrations of Power

Jesus taught the disciples to pray, *"For Yours is the kingdom and the power and the glory. Amen."* (**Matt. 6:13**). Jesus came to Earth as a man to reveal God as our heavenly Father—and the kingdom, the power, and the glory belong to Him. God's kingdom is the rule of heaven, power is the ability of heaven, and the glory is the atmosphere of heaven.

God is calling us to exercise His kingdom rule, demonstrate His power, and manifest His glorious presence on the kingdom of the Earth.

> Unfortunately, most of the church has been busy teaching religious traditions, with little demonstration of God's power

The way we demonstrate God's kingdom principles on Earth is to imitate Jesus. He carried the presence of God everywhere He went, and He demonstrated the kingdom in two essential ways.

1. Jesus *did* the works of the kingdom.

2. Jesus *taught* about the kingdom of heaven.

If we do not *teach* people about the kingdom, it will not advance. If we do not *do* the works of the kingdom, it will not be demonstrated with power.

Unfortunately, most of the church has been busy teaching religious traditions, with little demonstration of God's power (see **2 Tim. 3:5**)!

Be Like an Eagle

God's best gift is the power of choice. You can choose to be like a duck or like an eagle. If you get up in the morning expecting to have a bad day, you will rarely disappoint yourself.

Ducks quack and complain. Eagles soar above the crowd. Do not be like a duck, be an eagle!

BE BOLD to Declare:

* I will dominate temptation to sin, in Jesus' name.

* I will honor the Lord for every good gift from Heaven.

* I will dominate feelings of worry, doubt, and fear.

* I will dominate by living out of my spirit.

* I dominate things by faith in Christ.

Like an eagle in a storm, it is time for a Dominion Rising!

Chapter 2
Jesus Restored Dominion

> *"How God anointed Jesus of Nazareth with the Holy Spirit and with power, who went about doing good and healing all who were oppressed by the devil, for God was with Him."*
> **Acts 10:38**

Jesus demonstrated the dominion that Adam was supposed to walk in. He demonstrated the dominion that Adam had and came to earth to take back dominion from Satan.

Jesus, after His resurrection, restored the dominion that Adam had in the beginning—to all born-again believers.

The book of Matthew says,

> *"Jesus went about all the cities and villages, teaching in their synagogues, and preaching the gospel of the kingdom, and healing every sickness and every disease among the people."*
> **Matt. 9:35**

Every time you hear of the Gospel of the kingdom being preached, you always find healing of every sickness and disease.

Why? It is because healing demonstrates the Gospel of the kingdom. It is physical proof that the kingdom is near, or the kingdom is at hand, as the King James Version (KJV) says.

> *"But when he saw the multitudes, he was moved with compassion on them, because they fainted, and were scattered abroad, as sheep having no shepherd." "Then saith he unto his disciples, The harvest truly is plenteous, but the labourers are few,"* **Matt 9:36-37, KJV**

Let us look at these verses that says, *"Jesus went about all the cities and villages, teaching, preaching, and healing every sickness and every disease."* (**Matt. 9:35.**)

Who was doing the teaching, preaching, and healing? Jesus! Matthew goes on to say, *"Then saith He unto His disciples, 'The harvest truly is plenteous, but the laborers are few.'"* (**Matt. 9:37.**) He said that because He saw them, and He had compassion for them. He saw the multitude, saw that they were like sheep scattered, and He had compassion. He called His disciples together and said, "Listen guys, the harvest is ready, but we have so few laborers."

Now watch what scripture says: *"Pray ye therefore the Lord of the harvest, that he will send forth labourers into his harvest."* (**Matt. 9:38.**)

> *"And when he had called unto him his twelve disciples, he gave them power against unclean spirits, to cast them out, and to heal all manner of sickness and all manner of disease."* **Matt. 10:1**

It says, *"And when He had called unto Him His twelve disciples, He gave..."* If you look up the word *"gave"* it is a prolonged form of a primary Greek word *didōmi*. The verb is used as an alternate in most of the tenses meaning *to give*. It is pronounced *did'-o-mee*. It depends on how deep you go to what definition you come up with.

If you just look up Strong's Concordance, it is going to give you a basic understanding. You can go into it a little deeper if you use Thayer's.

When it said, "He *gave* them," it meant it was loaned, but later it was given as a possession. In the quote "He *gave* them power," read *loaned* to them.

The Greek word there for *power* is *exousia*, and it literally means *authority*. He gave them authority—what authority—the authority of Jesus.

It was the authority that Jesus was walking in. *"And He gave them authority against unclean spirits, to cast them out, and to heal all manner of sickness and all manner of disease."* Do you realize He was *giving* them, *loaning* them, the authority He Himself was operating? It was not less authority. It was the same authority. Now go down further,

> "*These twelve Jesus sent forth, and commanded them, saying, Go not into the way of the Gentiles, and into any city of the Samaritans enter ye not: "These twelve Jesus sent forth, and commanded them…"* **Matt. 10:5**

Notice He did not suggest, nor did He ask them. He commanded them saying, *"Go not into the way of the Gentiles, and into any city of the Samaritans enter ye not."* **(Matt. 10:5, KJV.)**

> *"But go rather to the lost sheep of the house of Israel. And as ye go, preach, saying, The kingdom of heaven is at hand. And as you go, preach."* **(Matt. 10:6-7, KJV.)**

The word for *preach* is the Greek work *kērussō*, and it means *proclaim*. The Greek even goes so far as to say,

> *"Proclaim with a liberty, a solemnity, and a gravity with which it must be listened to and obeyed. Proclaim, saying, 'The kingdom of heaven is at hand.'"* **Matt. 10:6-7**

Notice what He tells them in the next verse. Every time you see kingdom, the next thing you are going to see is this: *"Heal the sick, cleanse the lepers, raise the dead, cast out devils: freely ye have received, freely give."* (**Matt. 10:8.**)

If you can, get the picture of that! The closest picture we have is the one in our own minds when we think about heaven. I am talking about the place. If I could, I would give you a visual of that. If you were to walk down the streets of gold, would you see people on a crutch? No. Are you going to see a person in a wheelchair? No. You are not going to see people with any parts missing because they are going to be complete.

As It Is in Heaven

Why do we not see wheelchairs in heaven? Why do we not see missing body parts? Why do we not see crutches? Why do we not see people dying of Acquired Immunodeficiency Syndrome (AIDS) in heaven? That is because God's will is being done there.

If God's will is being done in heaven and you do not see any of those things there, and if He tells us to pray, *"Thy will be done on earth as it is in heaven,"* (**Matt. 6:10**), then we should not be seeing them here. Wherever you see sickness, you are not seeing God's will being done.

> The problem is: most of us stand around with our hands in our pockets instead of laying hands on the sick and speaking a blessing to everyone we meet.

Wherever you see God's will being done, you see empty wheelchairs, you see crutches laid on the ground, you see blind eyes open, and you see people exalting Jesus. (**Jn. 5:19.**)

Notice that today the church, the body of Christ, is always looking down the road waiting for the next revival, waiting for the next thing.

You must realize that the thing you need has already been given. It is just a matter of what you are going to do with it. Heaven is at hand, exactly as Jesus said, *"The kingdom of heaven is at hand."* The problem is: most of us stand around with our hands in our pockets instead of laying hands on the sick and speaking a blessing to everyone we meet.

I am going to go over this next part with you again. It says in Matthew,

> *"And when he had called unto him his twelve disciples, he gave them power against unclean spirits, to cast them out, and to heal all manner of sickness and all manner of disease."* **Matt. 10:1**

Jesus gave His twelve disciples authority against unclean spirits to cast them out, and to heal all manner of sickness and all manner of disease.

Do you realize He was using authority? He gave them authority and notice that He did not give specifics. It just says, *"He gave them authority against unclean spirits."* Why? *"…to cast them out."*

It did not matter 'which' unclean spirits, and it did not matter who had them. It did not matter how they got them. He just said that the unclean spirits had to go.

If it is a sickness or disease, it should be healed. Isn't that simple?

The problem is that we have made healing into a theology. We have made it into another sermon rather than into the freedom of the gospel.

Matthew said, *"Heal the sick, cleanse the lepers, raise the dead, cast out devils."* (**Matt. 8:10.**) Notice that all of those are right there together, even cleanse the lepers.

People say, "Well, there are not many lepers out today." It is not just about lepers; it is about the skin being cleansed and the blood being cleansed. It is about being cleansed from everything that is destroying.

In Luke, He says,

> *"Then he called his twelve disciples together, and gave them power and authority over all devils, and to cure diseases."*

> Notice the wording here, *"...and gave them power and authority over all devils, and to cure diseases."* **Lk. 9:1**

Jesus gave the disciples ability and the right to cast out any devil or to heal any sickness.

Again, notice the broad categories here: heal the sick and cure diseases, cleanse the lepers, raise the dead, cast out devils.

Most churches however focus on the person, asking questions like, "How did you get that way? What did you do? What sin did you commit? What problem do you have? How did you get this?"

I believe Jesus was saying, "Do not worry about how they got it. Do not focus on the person. Focus on the Kingdom." If you did focus on the Kingdom, what would this person look like?

Do you realize that when God looks at you, He treats you as He has faith in you? God is a faith God. He looks at us in faith. He believes we are actually going to be who He designed us to be and He treats us like that, even before we look like that. Even before anybody else would treat us that way, He looks at us and says, "I know what's in you."

It is like when Paul told Timothy, "I know what is in you. I know what you can do." Why? Paul said, "Because I put it there myself."

When the rest of the world is looking at you and saying, "I see how you are," God is saying, "I know what's in you. I know who you can be." Why? He is saying, "Quit looking at why or how a person got something and look at the kingdom." (See **2 Tim 1:6**.)

If you want to look at that person, picture them in heaven.

Would they be in that wheelchair? No.

God looks at people that way. He looks at that person in the wheelchair and says, "I will get one of My sons to pray for you, to lay hands on you; to put My life into you." God is looking for people that He can embody, that He can impart Himself into so that He can use them to impart Himself to other people.

He says here in Luke, *"And he sent them to preach the kingdom of God, and to heal the sick."* (**Lk. 9:2.**)

What did He send them to do? He sent them, *"to heal the sick."*

Kingdom equals deliverance. Kingdom equals freedom. Think about that. We have been delivered. The Scriptures say we have!

He has translated us from the power of darkness into the kingdom of Jesus (see **Col 1:13**).

He took you out of the power of darkness. When did He do that? It was when He put you in His Kingdom. When did you get into His Kingdom? That was when you were born again. The minute you were born again, the power of darkness had no power over you.

You were removed from its power and put into the Kingdom. You are now in the reign, the rule, and the supremacy of God's dear Son. You have been removed from the power of darkness.

If darkness is reigning in your life, it is there illegally!

BE BOLD to Declare:

* I will dominate and resist the spirit of selfishness.

* I will honor the Lord for all He accomplished on the day of His sacrifice.

* I will dominate and resist the fear of death.

* I speak 'to' problems, not about them.

Dominion is absolute authority, and is delegated by Jesus to believers.

Chapter 3
The Kingdom of Power

> *"The kingdom of God does not come with observation; nor will they say, 'See here!' or 'See there!' For indeed, the kingdom of God is within you."* **Lk. 17:20-21**

Many believers have heard messages taught about the kingdom of God, yet few have had a deep revelation of what it is. Therefore, most believers are missing the truth and benefits of the unseen kingdom of God.

God's kingdom is His sovereign government on earth. In the New Testament, the Greek word for "kingdom" is *basileia*, which means "royalty," "rule," "a realm." It comes from the root word *basileus*, which relates to the idea of a "foundation of power."

An earthly kingdom is the influence, dominion, will, and lordship of a king or prince over a certain territory and people.

The kingdom from heaven—the kingdom of God—is God's realm of power on earth. It is His dominion or lordship, in which He establishes His will through the finished work of Jesus in the lives of His people. God has established that His will and influence over the earth is to be accomplished by His people as guided by His Spirit. Spirit empowered believers should dominate and subdue sin, sickness, fear, poverty, demonic oppression, and all of Satan's works. *"The heaven, even the heavens, are the Lord's; But the earth He has given to the children of men."* (**Ps. 115:16.**)

"Then God blessed them, and God said to them, "Be fruitful and multiply; fill the earth and subdue it; have dominion over the fish of the sea, over the birds of the air, and over every living thing that moves on the earth." **Gen. 1:28**

God's Will Is Always Done in Heaven

God's will is <u>not</u> always done on the Earth. All you must do is watch the 6 o'clock news—and you hear of every sin, hatred, sickness, radical terrorism, and devil-inspired evil happening in the world today.

God's will is that empowered believers should receive and act upon the authority that Jesus won through His finished work at the Cross and at the whipping post. In this way, believers will demonstrate the power of God on the earth by healing the sick, casting out demons, and resisting the devil at every opportunity.

> The kingdom of God extends the dominion, power, and authority of Jesus to the Earth.

The kingdom of God extends the dominion, power, and authority of Jesus to the Earth.

The Holy Spirit Within

Instead of walking around moaning about how broke you are and how you cannot afford to give much to spread the gospel, you will start thinking about the fact that the One with the power to bring God's Word to pass is living inside you, and you'll change your tune. You will start saying things like, "God meets my needs according to His riches in glory, so I have plenty to meet my own needs and give to every good work!"

Then the Holy Spirit within you will go into action. He will give you plans, ideas, and inventions. He will open doors of opportunity, and then give you the strength and ability to walk through them.

Instead of sitting around wishing there was something you could do for your sick, unsaved neighbor, you will invite him into your house, tell him about Jesus, and then ask if you can pray for him. Always looking for an opportunity to lay hands on him fully expecting the Holy Spirit within you to release God's healing power and cause him to recover.

Instead of sitting around simply admiring the works of Jesus and reading about them each Sunday in church, you'll hit the streets and do those works yourself—and even greater works (see **Jn. 14:12**). You will stand up boldly and say:

> *"The Spirit of the LORD is upon Me, Because He has anointed Me, To preach the gospel to the poor; He has sent Me to heal the brokenhearted, To proclaim liberty to the captives And recovery of sight to the blind To set at liberty those who are oppressed; To proclaim the acceptable year of the LORD."* **Lk. 4:18-19**

More Than You Can Think

Wait a minute. Jesus spoke those words about Himself.

Yes, He did. However, He also said, *"...As my Father hath sent me, even so send I you."* (**Jn. 20:21**.)

You have been sent just like Jesus was (see **Rom. 8:29**). You have been sent to your family, your neighborhood, your workplace, your world to deliver the burden-removing, yoke-destroying power of God!

That is the reason God baptized you in the Holy Spirit. He intended for you to walk into a place and bring the power of God on the scene—the same power that enabled Samson to defeat the Philistines and make a fool out of the devil! The same power that enabled Elijah to call down fire from heaven and outrun the fastest horses in the country is what enabled Jesus to heal the sick, raise the dead, and calm the sea!

Can you imagine what all God could do in this earth if we would just become God-inside minded enough to let that power flow?

No, you cannot. As the Apostle Paul said, He is, *"able to do exceedingly abundantly above all that we ask or think, according to the power that works in us."* (**Eph. 3:20.**)

Maybe you have been waiting for God to do something in your life or in the lives of those around you. Maybe you have been saying, *"I know God is able to change this situation. I wonder why He does not do it?"* If so, read that last phrase again. It says He can do above what we can ask or think *according to the power that works in you!*

Start building your faith in that power. Instead of always gazing toward heaven saying, *"God, why do You not help me?"* look at yourself in the mirror and say, "The Spirit of God is living in me today and I expect Him to do wise, wonderful, amazing, and miraculous things through me!"

> A manifestation is when you "see and feel" what you believe.

Instead of meditating on your problems and natural inadequacies, get out your Bible and study the acts of the Holy Spirit from Genesis to Revelation. Start meditating on the power and sufficiency of the God who lives and walks within you every moment of every day!

When you begin to realize what a dynamite team you two really are, you will blast off into the realm of *exceeding above all* that you can ask or think—and the devil will never be able to catch you (see **Eph. 3:20**).

How to Speed Up Your Manifestation

Unbelievably, you can participate in speeding up your manifestation—OR slowing it down.

A manifestation is when you "see and feel" what you believe.

In the book of John, Jesus instructs us,

> *"He who has My commandments and keeps them, it is he who loves Me. And he who loves Me will be loved by My Father, and I will love him and **manifest Myself to him**."* **Jn. 14:21**

In Colossians, the apostle Paul instructs us *"Let the word of Christ **dwell in you richly** in all wisdom."* (**Col. 3:16.**)

The manifestation of what you believe for—is directly connected to what you store up in your heart and the words that you speak.

As children of God we can speak like God, *"who gives life to the dead and **calls those things** which do not exist as though they did,"* (**Rom 4:17-b.**)

Take every opportunity to **Prophesy:**

* I call my body healed.

* I call myself prosperous!

* I call myself disciplined.

* I call myself free from fear!

This illustrates the God kind of faith. God says things are so before there is physical proof that they are so. The same thing was done at creation (see **Gen. 1**). God spoke everything into existence, and then it was so. He spoke light into existence and then four days later created a source for that light to come forth, (see **Gen. 1:3, 14-19**).

God has given us the power to create with faith-filled words (see **Prov. 18:20-21, Mk. 11:14, 23**). If we are going to operate in God's kind of faith, we must learn to call those things that are not as though they were. (**Rom. 4:17b, KJV.**)

Your Word Level Matters

The measure of your Word level is the measure that will come back to you. *"For with the same measure that you use, it will be measured back to you."* (**Lk. 6:38-b.**)

In the book of Mark, Jesus instructed us *"Take heed what you hear. With "the same measure you use, it will be measured to you; and to you who hear, more will be given."* (**Mk. 4:24.**)

We all have the choice to be fixed on and filled-up with the Word—or to be fixed on the pain, lack, problem, and circumstances.

If your Word level is low, you can slow down or block your manifestation.

Give Attention to the Word

According to Proverbs, the Lord instructs us,

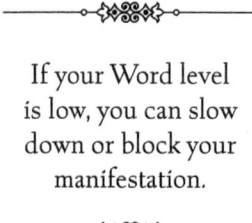

If your Word level is low, you can slow down or block your manifestation.

"give attention to my words; Incline your ear to my sayings. Do not let them depart from your eyes; Keep them in the midst of your heart; For they are life to those who find them, And health to all their flesh. Keep your heart with all diligence, For out of it spring the issues of life." **Prov. 4:20-23**

If you want to speed up your manifestation, you cannot be half-hearted or passive.

The "Easy" Way to Believe

In the Gospel of Matthew, we have a great way to believe and receive manifestations.

"Then behold, they brought to Him a paralytic lying on a bed. When Jesus saw their faith, He said to the paralytic, "Son, be of good cheer; your sins are forgiven you." And at once some of the scribes said within themselves, "This Man blasphemes!" But Jesus, knowing their thoughts, said, "Why do

*you think evil in your hearts? For **which is easier, to say,** 'Your sins are forgiven you,' or to say, 'Arise and walk'? But that you may know that the Son of Man has power on earth to forgive sins"—then He said to the paralytic, "Arise, take up your bed, and go to your house."* **Matt. 9:2-6**

In other words, Jesus demonstrated that anything and everything is 'easy' for the Lord God! *(He created the universe!)*

We should learn to SAY when confronted with a hard problem:

* That is easy for Jesus.

* With Christ in me, it is easy.

It seems that when we think just naturally, we say: this is so hard, or I am sick, or I cannot pay my bills.

Do Like Jesus Did

In the book of John Jesus told us what He did: *"Most assuredly, I say to you, the Son can do nothing of Himself, but **what He sees the Father do**; for whatever He does, the Son also does in like manner."* (**Jn. 5:19**.)

* Essentially, believers imitate Jesus (see **Eph. 5:1**), and He does the work.

* We speak 'to' the mountain (see **Mk. 11:23**) and He does the work. We 'abide' in the Word (see **Jn. 8:31-32; Jn. 15:7**) and He does the work.

* We lay hands on the sick (see **Mk. 16:17**) and He does the work.

The best way to speed up your manifestation is to study and meditate on God's promises and **refuse** to speak 'anything' **contrary** to what you believe!

Be Bold to Declare:

- On my good days, I am a child of God.

- On my difficult days, I am a child of God.

- In Christ, I have power over the enemy.

- I am eternally grateful for the love of Christ.

- I dominate thoughts of failure.

- I dominate thoughts of sorrow.

- I dominate depressing thoughts.

- I was created to have dominion.

You have dominion to soar above circumstances, like an eagle.

Chapter 4
KINGDOM BENEFITS ARE HERE

"Blessed be the God and Father of our Lord Jesus Christ, who hath blessed us with all spiritual blessings in heavenly places in Christ." (**Eph. 1:3.**)

Do you remember how God created the universe? He "spoke" and created everything! God's Word was activated to give people and the earth everything that would ever be needed.

Most Christians believe this and will agree that God, the Creator, is almighty and is awesome!

After God created everything, He created mankind and told them to take charge of His creation (see **Ps. 115:16**). At the very least, we should take charge of our own lives (see **Gen. 1:26**)!

For some, this truth is hard to understand. Jesus explained spiritual truth by comparing God's ways to planting a seed.

> *"The kingdom of God is as if a man should scatter seed on the ground, and should sleep by night and rise by day, and the seed should sprout and grow, he himself does not know how."* **Mk. 4:26-27**

We do not know how God's Word works, but you can have confidence that God is faithful to make sure His word comes to pass (see **Jer. 1:12.**).

Do you have needs that you would like God to do something about? Do you need the Lord to heal you? How about prosperity? How about deliverance from addictive habits? The truth is you do not need the Lord to do anything for you. He has already done His part. You have already got it, whatever "it" is.

Your part and my part are to "receive" what God has already done. This is when we activate the dominion power that God originally intended for mankind (see **Gen. 1:28; Matt. 16:18**).

This may sound crazy to some of you. You might be thinking, "But I have got a doctor's report to prove I do not have healing, or you have not seen my bank account." Regardless of what the natural facts are, the truth is that God has already provided whatever you need (see **Phil. 4:19; Matt. 6:33**).

Second Peter says,

> *"According as his divine power hath given unto us all things that pertain unto life and godliness, through the knowledge of him that hath called us to glory and virtue."* **2 Pet. 1:3**

The Only Thing Lacking is Knowledge

The Word of God says,

> *"Blessed be the God and Father of our Lord Jesus Christ, who hath blessed us with all spiritual blessings in heavenly places in Christ."* **Eph. 1:3**

What are these spiritual blessings? Salvation, grace, peace, joy, power, healing, deliverance, prosperity, hope, faith, protection, safety, Holy Spirit baptism, and gifts of the spirit.

Where are these spiritual blessings? In heavenly places. In other words, these blessings are already in the unseen spiritual realm.

Do you need to be saved? Yes! The First book of John says that, *"he is the propitiation for our sins: and not for ours only, but also for the sins of the whole world."* (**1 Jn. 2:2**.) He has already forgiven the sins of the entire world. It is not a matter of *if* God will forgive you; He has *already* forgiven sins. Will you receive His forgiveness? Will you put faith in what Jesus has done? That is the issue.

Many Christians receive this truth about salvation because we have been taught that salvation has already been given in heavenly places 2000 years ago. All Christians need to know that all of God's blessings were also given 2000 years ago by the finished work of Christ!

The scripture says He *"hath blessed us with all spiritual blessings,"* meaning it is already done. You already have all your spiritual blessings. Therefore, asking God or waiting on Him to bless you is hindering you from receiving what you need.

Yet the average Christian starts from an unbelieving position. If a believer is sick in their minds or bodies, they should start from the position of *"by His stripes, I was healed"* (**1 Pet. 2:24**) and *"I have the same power that raised Jesus from the dead living in me."* (**Eph. 1:19-20**.)

Many people take the doctor's report, google, media commercials, or the pain in their bodies and say, "I am sick. God, will You heal me?" They struggle *toward* victory instead of speaking *from* victory!

You might say, "I do not see the difference." There is a huge difference! Instead of defending your healing and receiving what Jesus already provided, some of us are trying to get God to do something He has not done yet. Nevertheless, He has already blessed us with everything we need!

We all need a fresh revelation of this truth. We get revelation knowledge by meditating on God's Word and will. Jesus has already provided everything you will ever need. You are blessed with all spiritual blessings—all of them!

Whether or not we see a physical manifestation of what He has done in the spiritual realm is dependent upon what we believe and how we act, not on what He has done. It is not up to the Lord to heal us; He has already healed us (see **1 Pet. 2:24**).

The Lord gave His miraculous power (dominion) for to us to "take" what is already in the spirit realm and bring it into the physical. (See **Matt 6:10**.)

Healing has already been provided. Financial prosperity has already been provided. Joy and peace and everything that you will ever need emotionally have already been provided. If you're having a down day, if things aren't going right, if you don't feel good — you don't need to embrace discouragement, despair, and hopelessness. And yet the average Christian just *embraces* this stuff, saying, "O God, I ask You to touch me. I ask You to give me joy."

Galatians 5:22-23, says *"love, joy, peace, longsuffering, gentleness, goodness, faith, meekness, and self-control"* are in you if you are born again. It is right there in your spirit! Most believers think it is a great request to ask for more love, joy, and peace. But that prayer assumes that it's God's fault that they don't 'feel' His love and joy.

The truth is, God has already poured out His love toward you. Look what it says here in Romans: *"The love of God is shed abroad in our hearts by the Holy Ghost which is given unto us."* (**Rom 5:5-b.**)

God loves you whether you feel it or not! His love has been poured in your heart—in other words, in your spirit. Moreover, His love is not conditional upon your good actions or holiness.

Again, go back to Ephesians, *"Blessed be the God and Father of our Lord Jesus Christ, who hath blessed us with all spiritual blessings in heavenly places in Christ." (Eph. 1:3.)*

Now, the scripture indicates those spiritual blessings are in heavenly places in Christ, but they are in you because *you* are in Christ, which is what the next verse says: *"According as he hath chosen us in him before the foundation of the world."* (**Eph. 1:4-a.**)

In the book of Philemon, another verse explains this truth. Paul was praying, *"that the communication of thy faith may become effectual"* (**Philemon 1:6**). That means that your faith would begin to work—*"by the acknowledging of every good thing which is in you in Christ Jesus."*

It is so wonderful to know, every good thing is in you in Christ! You already have it! Besides, He said He would never leave you nor forsake you (see **Heb. 13:5**). Thus, instead of praying, "Lord, just be with me this week, if it be Your will" or "O God, where are You? God, could You just love me? I do not feel the love of God."

> You do not need God to respond to you; you need to learn to respond to God!

Let us pray, "Thank You, Father, that You will never leave me, that You are always here with me. Thank You for Your goodness. Thank You for Your healing gift."

Start acknowledging the good things that the Word says is in you, and then your faith begins to be effective. You will start seeing these things "manifest" in your life. That is so much easier than begging and pleading with God to do something that He has already done!

When Jesus died on the cross, He said, *"It is finished."* (**Jn. 19:30**.) Additionally, the Scripture reveals in Ephesians that He is now seated at the Father's right hand (see **Eph. 1:20**). He is not working anymore. He has already done it. It is finished!

You do not need God to respond to you; you need to learn to respond to God! It is easier to defend something you already have than to go get something you do not have.

That is so powerful, but this is where so many Christians are missing it. They know that God can do all these things, but they do not think He has done anything yet. They start from a position of unbelief. They are crossways with the Word of God.

Regarding healing, the proper way to do it is to take Proverbs, *"Death and life are in the power of the tongue."* (**Prov. 18:21**.) Begin to release this dominion and power over sickness and disease: "I speak death to this sickness. I curse it and command it to leave. God, I speak the life that You have already put on the inside of me. I release it to flow through my body." This is how you start cooperating with God. Say it aloud!

We need to begin to believe that things have happened that we cannot see, taste, hear, smell, or feel.

We can believe that there are television and radio signals in the atmosphere, even though we cannot see them. We know that all we must do is take a television set, turn it on, tune it in, and we will see that those signals were there the whole time. Yet, we need to begin to apply this to spiritual things. We cannot limit this concept to just our physical realm.

There is more going on than just what you can perceive with your five senses. There is more than just your soulish, emotional realm. There is a spirit on the inside of you, and there is a spiritual realm, where God has already done His part.

If you do not receive revelation knowledge of Christ's finished work, you are going to be hit and miss in the Christian life.

You need to live from the standpoint that God has already done it. He has provided everything you need. It is not a matter of trying to get God to move in your life; it is a matter of you moving over into agreement with Him and receiving what He has already provided.

Why Does God's Creation Work That Way?

Unbelievably, you and I need to 'cooperate' with God for answers, healing, prosperity, and freedom from fear, doubt, worry, and addictions.

Let us say it another way: God needs us to cooperate with Him. Someone will say: "Oh no, God does not need anyone or anything—God controls everything that happens!"

In Matthew, Jesus said, *"Your heavenly Father knows that you need all these things."* (**Matt. 6:32.**)

If God already knows what we need, and God is good—then why do we need to pray or do anything?

Kingdom Benefits Are Here

Jesus instructed us to, *"seek first the Kingdom"* (**Matt. 6:33.**) and our needs would be supplied.

As children of God, we pray, do, and speak, with His authorization, and take dominion over the devil and problems.

Why does IT work that way? Because God gave dominion over the earth to people at the very beginning of creation (see **Gen 1:26-28**).

In the book of Ephesians, we were instructed: *"Now to Him who is able to do exceedingly abundantly above all that we ask or think, according to the power that works in us."* (**Eph. 3:20.**)

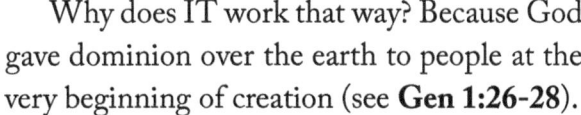

If you do not receive revelation knowledge of Christ's finished work, you are going to be hit and miss in the Christian life.

Now you have the answer to "why." God has chosen to work His power, *"according to the power that works in us."* (**Eph. 3:20-b.**)

Many believers do not learn this truth where they attend church.

Albert Einstein

One of the most brilliant minds on earth said, "The more I think I know, the less I really know."

We should all be humble enough to admit that we need to understand and learn more that God's plans are always good (see **Jas. 1:17; Jn. 10:10**).

This illustrates the God kind of truth. God says things are so before there is physical proof that they are so.

The same thing was done at creation (see **Gen. 1:3**). God spoke everything into existence, and then it was so. He spoke light into existence and then four days later created a source for that light to come from (see **Gen. 1:3, 14-19**).

God has given us the ability and responsibility to cooperate with His power (see **Prov. 18:20-21** and **Mark 11:23**).

If we are going to operate in God's kind of truth, we must learn that God's plan is good and that He gave us power of choice and of dominion. It is not what we think—it is how God created things to be.

God Cannot Lie

Psalm tells us how God guards His promises, *"My covenant I will not break, nor alter the word that has gone out of My lips."* (**Ps. 78:34.**)

Hebrews explains that, *"it is impossible for God to lie."* (**Heb. 6:18.**)

Therefore, we can be confident that when He gave mankind dominion over the earth—it is true forever!

The Lord God has established that He works 'through' believers—not apart from them. God works **with** us!

We take dominion over the devil and all His works by faith! We 'act' on the Word and speak the Word—and God supplies the power.

What's Our Part?

God supplies His grace and His power—believers supply the faith! Therefore: I am bold to declare:

* I will dominate temptation to sin, in Jesus' name.

* I will honor the Lord for every good gift from heaven.

* I will dominate feelings of worry, doubt, and fear.

* I will dominate and resist attacks of sickness, temptation, unbelief, and defeat, in Jesus' name.

Essentially, believers imitate Jesus (see **Eph. 5:1**), and He does the work.

We speak 'to' the mountain (see **Mk. 11:23.**) and He does the work.

We 'abide' in the Word (see **Jn. 8:31-32; Jn. 15:7**) and He does the work.

Essential Scriptures

Then God said,

> *"Let Us make man in Our image, according to Our likeness; let them have dominion over the fish of the sea, over the birds of the air, and over the cattle, over all the earth and over every creeping thing that creeps on the earth."* **Gen. 1:26**

> *"The heaven, even the heavens, are the LORD's; But the earth He has given to the children of men."* (**Ps. 115:16.**)

> *"You have made him to have dominion over the works of Your hands; You have put all things under his feet."* (**Ps. 8:6.**)

Dominion means destroying every yoke of bondage.
It's time to be skillful with God's promises!

Chapter 5
It Is Not a Faith Problem

"If you have faith as a mustard seed, you will say to this mountain, 'Move from here to there,' and it will move; and nothing will be impossible for you." (**Matt. 17:20.**)

I have heard several good Christian believers say, "I believe in God's miracles, His healing gifts, and how other people have been set free from addictions, oppression, and fear—but I just do not have that much faith."

Faith is a gift from God. We should especially notice that you were given the measure of faith (see **Rom. 12:3**), and you were given faith along with grace when you were born-again (see **Eph 2:8-9,**).In reviewing the scripture above, Matthew, believers only need faith like a mustard seed to do great things (see **Matt. 17**). We should also observe that the disciples had faith and were also given power over sickness and demons (see **Lk. 9:1-2, 10:9, 19**), but could not heal a boy with epilepsy.

This was a big question for the disciples. They had seen many successes before this one incident.

Jesus rebuked the demon, and it came out of him; and the child was cured that very hour. Then the disciples came to Jesus privately and said, *"Why could we not cast it out?"* Therefore, Jesus said to them, *"Because of your unbelief."* He did not say what some Christians say to hurting people, "You need more faith."

If you are a new creation in Christ, you have been given all the faith you will need to overcome circumstances. What we need is less unbelief!

Natural, sense-ruled thinking produces unbelief. In addition, unbelief cancels your faith. (**Mark 7:13.**)

What else adds to unbelief?

1. Searching Google about the symptoms of a specific disease.

2. Focusing on television (TV), Internet, news reports, media, and other people's negative experiences.

3. Considering any thought that is contrary to God's Word and His promises.

4. Unbelief is compounded when you do not get a manifestation of healing immediately.

We need to develop and strengthen our faith (see **Rom. 10:17**) and reduce the time we spend on things that will strengthen unbelief. We must live according to the Word and Spirit, not according to what we see, hear, and feel.

Personally, I believe what Jesus said, before I believe others or circumstances. Jesus said if you do not get results in prayer or speaking to a mountain size problem—it is because of unbelief!

Without faith, it is impossible to please God (see **Heb. 11:6**), so our relationship with the Lord is dependent on it. Faith is what brings the things God has provided for us from the spiritual realm into the physical realm (see **Heb. 11:1**). Our faith is the victory that enables us to overcome the world (sec **1 Jn. 5:4**). Everything the Lord does for us is accessed through faith.

One of the areas about faith that gives people the most trouble is the concept that we must acquire more faith and that some people have much faith, while others have virtually none. We spend a lot of effort,

It is Not a Faith Problem

like a dog chasing its tail, trying to get something we already have. Every born-again Christian already has the same quality and quantity of faith that Jesus has. That is awesome (see **Rom. 12:3-b**).

> Jesus said if you do not get results in prayer or speaking to a mountain size problem—it is because of unbelief!

In Ephesians, Paul says, *"For by grace are ye saved through faith; and that not of yourselves: it is the gift of God."* (**Eph. 2:8**.) It is God's grace that saves us, but not His grace alone. To be saved you must put faith in God's grace (see **Rom 10:8**).

The book of Romans says, *"God ... calleth those things which be not as though they were."* (**Rom. 4:17-b**.) God's kind of faith operates supernaturally, beyond the limitations of our natural faith.

The context of this verse from Romans speaks about how God supernaturally blessed Abram and Sarai with a child in their old age. Abram was 100 and Sarai was 91 when Isaac was born. The year before Isaac's birth, when Abram still did not have a child by his wife, God told them the child was coming, and He changed Abram's name to Abraham and Sarai's name to Sarah. Abram meant "high father," but Abraham means, "To be populous, father of a multitude." God changed Abram's name and called him the father of a multitude before it came to pass. The Epistle to the Romans explains this action by saying that, *"God calleth those things which be not as though they were."* (**Rom. 4:17**.)

New Creations Have Power

Even brand-new believers who have confessed Jesus as Savior and believe in their heart that Jesus was raised from the dead (see **Rom. 10:9**)—have all the faith they need (see **Lk. 17:6**).

* God's power is in His Word (see **Heb. 1:3**).

* God's Word gives you power to overcome every attack of the enemy (see **Jas. 4:7**).

* Change your thoughts and you can change your life (see **Rom. 12:2**).

* With God's power you can change the impossible to possible (see **Mk. 9:23**).

* With God's Word of power, you can change defeat into victory (see **1 Jn. 5:4**).

* You can change doubt into faith.

* You can change stress into peace.

* If you are in a fight—fight to win (see **1 Tim. 6:12**).

As believers, we have spiritually powerful plans for our lives that we can "prove" if we will totally yield ourselves to God.

> *"Do not be conformed to this world, but be transformed by the renewing of your mind, that you may prove what is that good and acceptable and perfect will of God."* **Rom 12:2**

One scripture that is widely misunderstood about faith is:

> *"For I say, through the grace given unto me, to every man that is among you, not to think of himself more highly than he ought to think; but to think soberly, according as God hath dealt to every man the measure of faith."* **Rom. 12:3, KJV**

We may have different gifts, but they are not better than someone else. Paul then continued in Romans, with the word "for," and drew a comparison from the way our bodies have different parts, but they all work together to make one body. *"For as we have many members in one body, but all the members do not have the same function."* (**Rom. 12:3**.)

Religion has interpreted this verse (see **Rom. 12:3**) to say that we should think of ourselves in a lowly manner, but that is not what Paul was saying. It would be proper to say that we should not think of ourselves more highly or lower than we ought to. We need to remember that any good thing we have is a gift from God (see **1 Cor. 4:7**). Paul was admonishing us to have the correct viewpoint, not a lowly viewpoint.

Paul said we must remember that God has given every believer the measure of faith. This sobers us up because we recognize that what we have is a gift from God that every child of God possesses. Some of us live up to more of our potential than others are, but it is only God's mercy that makes it possible for any of us to accomplish anything.

God has dealt to every person "the" measure of faith, not "a" measure of faith. There are not different measures with God. The Lord does not give one-person great faith while another person is given small faith. We were all given an equal amount of faith at salvation. The problem is not that we do not have faith, but rather we do not know how to use our faith, because of a lack of renewing our minds.

Peter said we had "like precious faith" with him (see **2 Pet. 1:1**). The same faith that he used to raise Dorcas from the dead (see **Acts 9:36-42**) is in us too. The same faith that Peter used is the same faith that we have.

Paul said he was living his Christian life by the faith of the Son of God (see **Gal. 2:20**). Since we all have been given "the" measure of faith, then that means we all have the faith of the Son of God in us. Our faith is sufficient. The problem we are experiencing is a result of our minds not knowing what we have.

In the same way that a car battery transfers its power to the starter through battery cables, so our minds are what allows this faith of God that is in our spirits to flow into our bodies. If our minds are not renewed, then it is like having corroded cables. The power is there, but it will not flow. Likewise, we believers have the same faith that Jesus has, but it will not flow through us until we renew our minds through the Word of God (see **Rom, 8:29**).

The Requirement of Dominion

In the beginning, God breathed life into Adam (see **Gen. 2:3**). Therefore, Adam was Spirit-filled! Although, soon died spiritually by disobeying God, bowed his knee to Satan, and gave away his dominion to the deceiver.

Do not worry, God already had a plan to give back dominion to mankind, because Satan is a thief. God always declares the end from the beginning and He prophesied that the Savior would come to restore man's dominion (see **Isa. 46:10**). Dominion rightfully belongs to man. Jesus came to earth to destroy the works of Satan (see **1 Jn. 3:8**) and to restore the pathway for the Spirit of God to once again dwell within those who will believe and receive (see **Ezek. 36:26**).

To this extent, for man to walk in the dominion that Adam had—man must have the Spirit of God within. Whereby, Jesus, being the last Adam, is the very one that will baptize believers with the Holy Spirit (see **Mk. 1:8**).

Dominion operates by faith. Do not misunderstand, I can do nothing of myself, unless I am 'in Christ.'

Chapter 6
Dunamis Power

"You shall receive power when the Holy Spirit has come upon you." **Acts 1:8**

You have been involved with the Holy Spirit since you first accepted Jesus as your Lord and Savior.

When you prayed a sincere prayer according to Romans and confessed that Jesus was raised from the dead to give you salvation; the Holy Spirit performed the miracle of the "new birth" in your spirit (see **Rom. 10:9**).

The first letter to the Corinthians states that no one says "Jesus is Lord" except by the Holy Spirit (see **1 Cor. 12:3**).

Jesus Himself told the men who walked by His side for 3 years that it is to their "advantage" if He went away and sent them the Holy Spirit (see **Jn. 16:7**).

Just think of that!

Would you like the inside information that will guide you through the bad news and uncertainties of this world?

All you must do is ask the Father in Jesus' name to be filled with the Holy Spirit. Your only job is to believe and receive—and Jesus has promised to baptize you with the overflowing "rivers of living water" power of the Holy Spirit (see **Jn. 7:37-39**)! It is Jesus who baptizes you with the Holy Spirit. (**Matt. 3:11.**)

> *"So I say to you, ask, and it will be given to you; seek, and you will find; knock, and it will be opened to you. For everyone who asks receives, and he who seeks finds, and to him who knocks it will be opened. If a son asks for bread from any father among you, will he give him a stone? Or if he asks for a fish, will he give him a serpent instead of a fish? Or if he asks for an egg, will he offer him a scorpion? If you then, being evil, know how to give good gifts to your children, how much more will your heavenly Father give the Holy Spirit to those who ask Him!"* **Lk. 11:9-13**

The Power of the Holy Spirit in You

Believers today have vastly underestimated the power of the Holy Spirit. You may wonder how I can be so sure of that. It is simple, really. If we truly understood and believed what the Bible tells us about Him, we would never worry about anything again. All hell has to offer could come against us and we would not fear. We would just grin and say, "Bring it on, devil! God lives within me, and He has given me all the wisdom, strength, power, and provision I need to crush you like a bug."

Right now, you may think you could never have that kind of boldness. However, let me ask you something: What would you do if Jesus appeared to you today? How would you act if He linked His arm in yours and told you that from now on, He would be physically present with you in every situation? If you became sick, He would lay His hand on you, and you would be healed. If you ran short of money, He would pray and multiply your resources. If you encountered a problem, and you did not know how to handle it, He would tell you exactly what to do.

Under those circumstances, you would be very bold and confident, would you not? Every time you ran into trouble, you would just glance over at Jesus standing next to you and suddenly, you would have great courage.

Of course, there is one problem. The fact is you do not have that advantage. You do not have Jesus standing next to you in the flesh taking care of your every need.

Although, you do have something *better*.

I realize it is difficult to believe there is anything more beneficial than Jesus' physical presence. Nevertheless, there is. Jesus said so Himself.

That is right. In the hours just before He was crucified, He told His disciples that He would be leaving them and returning to His Father in heaven. When they expressed their sorrow and dismay, He said:

> *"And I will pray the Father, and He will give you another Helper, that He may abide with you forever—the Spirit of truth, whom the world cannot receive, because it neither sees Him nor knows Him; but you know Him, for He dwells with you and will be in you"..."Nevertheless I tell you the truth. It is to your advantage that I go away; for if I do not go away, the Helper will not come to you; but if I depart, I will send Him to you,"* **John 14:16-17, 16:7**

To grasp the impact of this last statement fully, you must realize that Jesus was talking to a group of men who had followed Him day and night for three years. They had seen His miracles. They had enjoyed perfect protection and provision at His hand.

Peter was sitting there among them. Can you not just imagine what was running through his mind? No doubt, he was thinking of the first time Jesus had borrowed his boat. After He had finished preaching from it, He had said to Peter, "Grab your nets and we'll go catch some fish." It was the middle of the day. Peter knew you could not catch fish in the daylight in that lake—the water was too clear. The fish would see the net and run from it.

Even though, just to humor Him, Peter had done what Jesus said and ended up with a net-busting, boat-sinking load of fish. What a day!

Then there was the time Jesus healed Peter's mother-in-law of a deadly fever—cured her instantly!

Even that did not hold a candle to what happened on the Mount of Transfiguration. That day Peter had seen Moses and Elijah talking with Jesus. He had watched His body transfigure before his very eyes. He had seen the shining cloud of glory and heard the awesome voice of Almighty God!

As those events passed through Peter's mind, he must have wondered, "How can it possibly be expedient or to my "advantage" for Jesus to go away?"

Knowing that question was in the heart of every one of His disciples, Jesus said, in essence,

> *"I know this is hard for you to believe but trust Me on this. I'm not lying to you. It's better for you if I go away so that I can send the Holy Spirit to not only be with you, but to be in you!"* **Jn. 14:17**

The Power of God

It has been more than 2,000 years since Jesus foretold the importance of the Holy Spirit—and most of us are still struggling to believe it fully.

Theologically, we know it is true, and we thank God that we are born again and baptized in the Holy Ghost. Then, we open our mouths and say things like, "If I could just feel Jesus' hand on my forehead, it would be easier for me to receive my healing."

Why is that?

I believe it is because we have not truly appreciated the might and the ministry of the Holy Spirit. We have not yet had a full revelation of Who this is that is living inside us.

Many Christians, for example, seem to think the first time the Holy Spirit did much of anything was on the Day of Pentecost. However, that is not true. The Holy Spirit has been at work on this planet ever since the beginning.

Look at the Book of Genesis and you can see that for yourself. There in the first few verses we find:

> *"In the beginning God created the heaven and the earth. And the earth was without form, and void; and darkness was upon the face of the deep. And the spirit of God moved upon the face of the waters. And God said, Let there be light: and there was light,"* **Gen. 1:1-3**

Think about that! The Holy Spirit was hovering, waiting to supply the power to create. Then the moment God spoke the Word, *"Light be!"* (literal Hebrew translation), the Spirit sprang into action and supplied the power to bring this universe into being.

That is how the Bible introduces us to the Holy Spirit!

You see, the Holy Spirit is the power of God. Every time you see God's power in action, you can be sure the Holy Spirit is on the scene.

When the Holy Spirit came on Samson, he single-handedly killed a thousand Philistine soldiers (see **Judg. 15:14-16**). Can you imagine how embarrassing that must have been for the Philistines who escaped?

Some people get the idea that Samson was able to do those great exploits because he was a giant of a man. However, he was just an ordinary fellow. He only became extraordinary when the Spirit of God came on him.

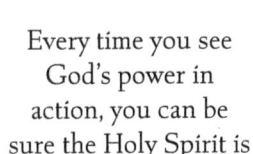

Every time you see God's power in action, you can be sure the Holy Spirit is on the scene.

The prophet Elijah was the same way. On his own, he was just as normal as you and me. He was once so frightened by the threats of a woman that he hid in the wilderness and asked God to kill him so he would not have to face her.

Nevertheless, when the Holy Spirit came on him, Elijah was a powerhouse. He once called down fire from heaven, killed 400 prophets of Baal, and outran the king's chariot (drawn, no doubt, by the fastest horses in the nation of Israel). Moreover, he did it all in one day (see **1 Kin. 18-19**).

The Most Amazing Mind!

Do not get the idea from those examples that the Holy Spirit is simply a mindless source of raw power—far from it! When He moves in on a situation, He does it with wisdom and understanding so vast that it staggers the human mind.

Isaiah says of Him: *"Who hath directed the spirit of the Lord, or being his counselor hath taught him?"* (**Isa. 40:13**) Now go back to the prior verse, which further explains:

> *"Who hath measured the waters in the hollow of his hand, and meted out heaven with the span, and comprehended the dust of the earth in a measure, and weighed the mountains in scales, and the hills in a balance?"* **Isa. 40:12**

Consider for a moment what kind of mind could take a handful of water, weigh it, and then compute all the moisture changes of the earth that would take place over untold thousands of years.

What kind of mind could take a handful of dust, weigh it, and then figure out how to form the earth—mountains and all—in such a way that it would always stay in perfect balance?

That is the kind of mind the Spirit of God has!

When He put this earth together, He did it so perfectly that it could travel 1,000 miles an hour in one direction and 10,000 miles an hour in another, both at the same time, without ever getting the slightest degree off course. He constructed it so that it could compensate for all the movement of the tides and all the use and abuse it would receive at the hands of man and still make its way through the heavens exactly on time.

Listen, this is the One who is planning your life! This is the One who dwells within you and walks within you. When you join yourself to the Lord, you become one spirit with Him (see **1 Cor. 6:17**). In addition, He does not change or shrink up His abilities so He could fit them inside you.

No, if you are a born-again, Holy Spirit-baptized believer, He is everything *in you* that He has ever been. He has the same awesome power. He has the same astounding ability to compute, to comprehend and plan in infinite detail everything that has ever been—everything that now is—and everything that ever will be!

What is more, when you run into something you cannot handle and you call on Him for help, He is not a million light years away. He is right there inside you! He is ready to supply you with whatever you need.

He is ready to be your comforter. He is ready to be your teacher and your trainer. He is ready to be your advocate, your standby, your counselor. He is ready to put His supernatural power and mind to work for you 24 hours a day.

A Perfect Gentleman

"Well then, why has He not helped me before now?" you ask. "Heaven knows I have needed it!"

He has been waiting for you to give Him something He can work with. He has been waiting there inside you just as He hovered over the face of the waters in Genesis, waiting for you to speak the Word of God in faith.

That has been His role since the beginning–to move on God's Word and deliver the power necessary to cause that Word to manifest in the earth. That is what He did at creation...and that is what He is commissioned to do for you.

Nonetheless, remember, He is your helper, not your dominator. If you are walking around talking doubt, unbelief, and other worthless words, He is severely limited. He will not slap His hand over your mouth and say, "I do not care what you say, I am going to bless you anyway."

No, the Holy Spirit is the perfect gentleman. He will never force anything on you. He will just wait quietly for you to open the door for Him to work.

In such manner, decide right now to start opening that door. Develop an awareness of the reality of the Holy Spirit within you. Stop spending all your time meditating on the problems you are facing and start spending it meditating on the power of the One inside you Who can solve the problems. In other words, start becoming more God-inside minded!

Do you know what will happen if you do that? All heaven will break loose in your life.

BE BOLD to Declare:

* I will dominate temptation to sin, in Jesus' name.

* I will honor the Lord for every good gift from heaven.

* I will dominate feelings of worry, doubt, and fear.

* I dominate thoughts of sickness.

* I dominate and cast down discouraging thoughts.

* I dominate and resist the devil.

* I'm living out of my spirit.

Jesus did not pray for people to be healed, or pray for freedom from demonic oppression. Jesus used dominion to command healing and freedom.

Chapter 7
POWERED BY THE SPIRIT

"He will baptize you with the Holy Spirit and fire."
(Matt. 3:11-c)

I pray and sing "in the spirit" every day. I surrender my own will to the leading and teaching of the Holy Spirit—and begin to pray privately with a wonderful heavenly, unknown tongue.

Does that surprise you?

No matter where we are on planet earth, we can enter the "secret place" of prayer to the 'Most High God'—in the wonderful name of Jesus—where the Holy Spirit gives powerful holy sounds, syllables, and spiritual words. It's the true worship *"in the spirit."*—that our Lord Jesus taught about (see **Jn. 4:23-24** and **1 Cor. 14:14**).

It is the same phrase used by the apostles Paul and John. It is a private, supernatural prayer to the Heavenly Father, through the Holy Spirit, in Jesus' mighty, holy name.

Humbling ourselves "in the presence of the Lord" is one the most awesome things we can experience on planet earth!

Have We Resisted the Wrong Thing?

Do not misunderstand. At first, I did not want this to happen to me. I was just like a lot of other Christians that are discouraged (by well-meaning church leaders) from receiving something thought to be unnatural and not normal. The truth is that it is supernatural!

When I heard the good news that the Holy Spirit is alive and well on planet earth, I was amazed and very hungry to find out more! You see living a normal, natural life is just conforming to what society, organized religion, and the 6 o'clock news tells us.

Should we not be living by what Heaven tells us?

It's sad to see that many well-meaning Christians are living the "same ole, same ole" life—waking up to another day of going to work, coming home, and watching TV—then praying for the weekend, to get some temporary desires satisfied.

What if life could be an exciting adventure every day?

What if we could live life in a super-natural way—doing the works of Jesus, helping people with faith-filled words, and healing from heaven?

We can! We can soar much higher than our physical senses can take us. *(Jesus promised that we could.)*

It is Better If I Go Away

The disciples of Jesus were eyewitnesses to the most phenomenal and glorious miracles the world has ever seen!

The disciples were amazed as blind eyes were opened and the dead were raised to life. The disciples heard Jesus command a raging storm to die and a fig tree to wither. They saw thousands fed as Jesus multiplied a few fish and loaves of bread. The words of many prophets of God were coming to pass right before their very eyes!

Never had mankind witnessed the miraculous hand of God in such an overwhelming and personal way.

Yet, as wonderful as things seemed to be—the disciples were told by Jesus Himself that it would be better if He went away. He said that the Heavenly Father had a far more excellent plan for them—and it would be to their "advantage" if He returned to heaven (see **Jn. 16:7**).

The Holy Spirit Is Waiting On You

You are not an accident. God has a divine plan for your life, and this great plan will be fulfilled as you are led by the power of the Holy Spirit!

The number one thing you and I need to know is that God cares about you. He loves you!

> *"For I know the thoughts that I think toward you, says the LORD, thoughts of peace and not of evil, to give you a future and a hope. Then you will call upon Me and go and pray to Me, and I will listen to you. And you will seek Me and find Me, when you search for Me with all your heart,"*
> **Jer. 29:11-13**

The second thing that we should all realize is that *"God is on our side,"* we do not have to fear the unseen, supernatural world if we trust our Creator (see **Ps. 118:6**).

The "Unseen" World Is Real

If we are going to trust in the Lord for a blessed life, then one vital fact should be settled in our thinking: The "unseen" world is more real than the seen world—and this supernatural world has a dramatic effect on everything that happens in the "seen" world.

In the unseen world there are angelic spirits and demonic spirits, there is a real heaven and a real hell—and of course there is the unseen Lord God Himself, Creator, and Sustainer of everything!

Another thing to remember when you are praying to receive the "secret power of God, the Holy Spirit," is that He is a gentleman and will never force you—but always waits until you open your heart to choose Him.

Your spirit—your heart—the "hidden man of the heart"—the eternal you on the inside—has been made in the image of God.

You might be thinking: *"That does not sound like what I have heard in my church."*

You are right—usually, the only time we hear anything about the unseen world is at funerals. Do you want to wait until your funeral to find out if there is really an invisible world?

The Bible definition of faith is that it is the substance and evidence of things that cannot be seen.

"Everyone" Has Faith in The Unseen

Everyone has faith and everyone believes...something.

What about your actions when the weather predictions are indicating a major storm might be heading your way? You look outside and it is a clear day, yet you start making plans to take cover, relocate, or board everything up. By faith, you start acting based on what you have been told.

Most of our everyday activities are done by faith.

Do you wake up every morning and head toward your car by faith, believing that it will start and get you to work? It is something that you cannot see while you are in the shower, but your evidence is that the mechanic said the vehicle was tuned up and ready to go.

The Bible definition of faith is that it is the substance and evidence of things that cannot be seen.

What do you do when your boss tells you that a firing is about to take place if you do not get to work? By faith, you believe it and get back to work. Your evidence? The person that used to sit next to you until last week is not there anymore.

You cannot see the air you breathe (I am not talking about polluted air). Still, there is "unseen" evidence that air is flowing through your lungs, and you are alive!

You cannot see atomic or hydrogen molecules, but we believe that our world is in danger every day because of "nuclear" weapons. The evidence—we have been given detailed physical evidence by reputable news reporters, scientists, and historians.

Human beings were created to live by faith.

> *"For since the creation of the world His invisible attributes are clearly seen, being understood by the things that are made, even His eternal power and Godhead, so that they are without excuse."* **Rom. 1:20**

Help From Heaven

It is imperative that we get an understanding that there is an unseen world all around us.

If you are searching for the safest way to live in this violent world, and are not satisfied with typical religious thinking, you must know how to get help from Heaven.

Satan is alive and well on Earth. He makes himself visible by every evil manifestation that you can see.

The works of the devil are obvious in every corner of the world, in every news broadcast, in every mental institution, in every devil-worshipping cult, and in every poverty-stricken, third-world country. However, I do not want to give "the salesman of fear" any more press. What we need is to magnify the goodness of Almighty God. God is love. He offers hope, supernatural protection, and gives real peace to overcome the evil of this world.

In light of the many examples in God's Word (Jesus, Noah, Abraham, David, Daniel, Shadrack, Joshua, Moses, Elijah, Peter, and Paul), we can expect supernatural protection. God's promises belong to us. It is not because of anything we have done. It is entirely because of what Jesus has done.

Are there conditions to God's protection—absolutely.

Have we fulfilled all the conditions—not by a long shot.

We have a long way to go to get ourselves to believe what God has promised. However, we can get there!

Believe Before You See

Remember the Lord's Prayer? *"Thy will be done on earth as it is in Heaven."* Jesus was calling for God's will, from the unseen heaven, to be done in the earth. In the book of James, we are taught that, *"every good and perfect gift comes down from the Father of Lights,"* (**Jas. 1:17**.)

Consequently, our prayers are calling for God's goodness in the "unseen" world of Heaven, to manifest in our "seen" world.

Having said that, we should also consider that human nature is to say; *"I will believe it when I see it."*

Granting, the truth is that we need to believe "first."

If there was ever a generation where people need to be aware of God's "unseen" world and know how things operate there, it is this generation.

You will never understand the truth of God's Creation, His ways, His Word—unless you submit your own will and ways to God's Will and ways.

It is a "Hidden" Secret

The most wonderful promises of God are reserved especially for "you"—the born again, Spirit-filled believer!

> *"Attaining to all riches of the full assurance of understanding, to the knowledge of the mystery of God, both of the Father and of Christ, In whom are hidden all the treasures of wisdom and knowledge,"* **Col. 2:2-b-3**

It is the "unsearchable riches of Christ" that "unbelievers" cannot understand. Our preaching of the Good News is to, *"make all see what is the fellowship of the mystery, which from the beginning of the ages has been hidden in God who created all things through Jesus Christ,"* (**Eph. 3:9.**)

The wonderful mysteries of the goodness of God are hidden from the devil, enemies of the cross, and anyone who practices evil.

> *"But we speak the wisdom of God in a mystery, the hidden wisdom which God ordained before the ages for our glory. Which none of the rulers of this age knew; for had they known, they would not have crucified the Lord of glory."* **1 Cor. 2:7-8**

Granting, as it is written:

> *"Eye has not seen, nor ear heard, Nor have entered into the heart of man the things which God has prepared for those who love Him. But God has revealed them to us through His Spirit. For the Spirit searches all things, yes, the deep things of God."* **1 Cor. 2:9-10**

The only enemy of the eagle is the serpent. The eagle has the ability to grab the serpent and rise high, to send the serpent to its death.
* You have dominion over Satan.

Chapter 8
Dominion in Action

*"For whom He foreknew, He also **predestined** to be **conformed** to the image of His Son, that He might be the firstborn among many brethren."* (**Rom. 8:29**)

Here are the two steps needed to activate the dominion and authority that Jesus wants believers to walk in: First, get delivered and then get discipled.

If you get discipled and are truly a disciple of Christ, you are not going to be doing anything that would allow the devil to have power and authority in your life.

Isn't that simple? You are removed from Satan's power and his authority. You might be thinking, "Well I thought he did not have any authority." Satan only has the authority in the world that 'we' give him.

The Bible says in the First Epistle of John, *"We know that we are of God, and the whole world lies under the sway of the wicked one."* (**1 Jn. 5:19.**)

"The whole world lies under the sway of the wicked one." It lies under the power of the wicked. The only thing Satan has is his deception, which is to keep you in bondage and make you think, "Well, I am just a bad person. I did "this or that, so I deserve cancer. I deserve …" No! You do not deserve that.

Notice that in Luke it said, *"He sent them to preach the Kingdom of God, and to heal the sick."* (**Lk. 9:2.**)

Luke says, *"And the seventy returned again with joy, saying, Lord, even the devils are subject unto us through thy name."* (**Lk. 10:17.**)

In Matthew, the man with the lunatic son came to Jesus and said, *"Lord, I brought my son to your disciples and they could not cure him."* (**Matt. 17:13.**) Jesus rebuked the devil, and the devil departed out of the child, and he was cured from that very hour.

In the book of Matthew, it goes on to say,

> *"And when they were come to the multitude, there came to him a certain man, kneeling down to him, and saying, Lord, have mercy on my son: for he is lunatic, and sore vexed: for ofttimes he falleth into the fire, and oft into the water. And I brought him to thy disciples, and they could not cure him. Then Jesus answered and said, O faithless and perverse generation, how long shall I be with you? how long shall I suffer you? bring him hither to me. And Jesus rebuked the devil; and he departed out of him: and the child was cured from that very hour."* **Matt. 17:14-19**

In Matthew, there was the question from the disciples asking why they could not cast the devil out of the man's son.

> *"Then came the disciples to Jesus apart, and said, Why could not we cast him out? What was the answer Jesus gave them? And Jesus said unto them, Because of your unbelief: for verily I say unto you, If ye have faith as a grain of mustard seed, ye shall say unto this mountain, Remove hence to yonder place; and it shall remove; and nothing shall be impossible unto you."* **Matt. 17:20**

He answered their question by saying, *"It was because of your unbelief."* In other words, they could have done it by faith. Matthew will answer why there was such a question:

Dominion in Action

> *"And it came to pass, that when Jesus had finished these parables, he departed thence. And when he was come into his own country, he taught them in their synagogue, insomuch that they were astonished, and said, Whence hath this man this wisdom, and these mighty works? Is not this the carpenter's son? is not his mother called Mary? and his brethren, James, and Joses, and Simon, and Judas? And his sisters, are they not all with us? Whence then hath this man all these things? And they were offended in him. But Jesus said unto them, A prophet is not without honor, save in his own country, and in his own house. And he did not many mighty works there because of their unbelief."* **Matt. 13:53-58**

We read in Luke where he had already sent them out (see **Lk. 10:19**). If you look at the chronology of this, Luke came before Matthew, so Jesus had sent them out and they had come back and said, "Lord, even devils are subject to us through Your name." Why? It was because He had given them power and authority. We could say that it was ability and dominion.

The Greek word *dunamis* (pronounced *doo'-nam-is*) was translated *power*. It was defined like an explosion, miraculous power. It was a gift filled with power. When they were out demonstrating this power, the atmosphere was like a celebration. They were happy, they were excited, and they were coming back all pumped up.

When you go back to where the scripture said, "And He gave them power," it really meant that He "loaned them power." Why?—because it was for a specific mission. (Not like on the day of Pentecost.)

He loaned it to them, and He said, "You go and do this."

After they came back, and that man brought his son, that mission was over, so the power was gone. Why?—because it was on loan. It did not come to stay until the book of Acts. They were so used to saying, "Devil, come out," and BAM! The devil would come out. They thought, "Hey! That was easy."

Then this man came up and they tried to cast the devil out, but the power was not there. Think about that. That power was not there. They were trying to operate in a gift, but the gift was not there. Jesus said they could have done it by faith, not by a gift.

Do you see the difference?

If you think about it, you will see that it opens so much more to you because you start to realize that there are times when you will operate by a gift and there are other times when you just must go by faith. Once you realize that, suddenly you will see how that opens things up.

In Matthew, they did not have power beyond their unbelief (see **Matt. 17:14-20**). Nevertheless, just because there was not power does not mean they were not responsible for getting it done. They still had to get it done, but they had to operate by faith instead of by power.

He said, in Luke,

> *"And the seventy returned again, with joy, saying, Lord, even the devils are subject unto us through thy name." "And he said unto them, I beheld Satan as lightning fall from heaven. Behold, I give unto you power to tread on serpents and scorpions, and over all the power of the enemy: and nothing shall by any means hurt you."* **Lk. 10:17**

"Behold," look or take notice, "I give unto you..." What was he giving to them? He was giving them *exousia*, "*authority* to tread on serpents and scorpions, and over all the *power*, (a word taken from the root word *dunamis, meaning the ability)*, of the enemy."

Notice He did not say, "I give you power." He did not say I am giving you ability. He said, "I am giving you *authority*." The reason He did not say, "I am giving you ability," is because the ability did not come until later, but they could still have gotten it done through authority. Authority relies on faith, but ability relies on the gift or the *dunamis (inherent or manifested power)* of the Holy Spirit. "And nothing shall by any means hurt you."

Luke 10:20, *"Notwithstanding in this rejoice not, that the spirits are subject unto you; but rather rejoice, because your names are written in heaven."*

Let us tie this together. What were they doing? We started in Genesis, talking about man having dominion (see **Gen. 1:26-28**). Jesus comes. He is not under the authority of Satan, so He is operating in the dominion that God gave man in the beginning.

The Bible calls Jesus the Last Adam. There is the first Adam and there is the Last Adam. Jesus was not the Second Adam; He was the Last Adam. You must realize that.

That means that you have dominion. God gave Adam dominion, then Adam gave it to Satan, then Jesus showed up as the Last Adam. He then gave His disciples authority to operate. Jesus was not operating under Satan's authority.

Jesus Gave Us 'His' Authority

John says, *"But as many as received him, to them gave He power to become the sons of God, even to them that believe on his name:"* (**Jn. 1:12.**)

Have you received Him?

He gave you and me authority.

> *"But ye shall receive power, after that the Holy Ghost is come upon you: and ye shall be witnesses unto me both in Jerusalem, and in all Judaea, and in Samaria, and unto the uttermost part of the earth."* **Acts 1:8**

Notice, they were given authority in John. It says, *"...to as many as received Him"* (**Jn. 1:12.**) Ability came later.

Jesus loaned it to them for a while, but we know in Acts, it came and stayed so that they could get born again (see **Acts 2:1-4.**). When the Spirit came, it came to stay. Before that, God's people had power that came and went, just like the Old Testament prophets had.

However, under the New Testament, we have the power that came to stay. Jesus said, "I am going to go. If I do not go, I cannot send the Comforter." This He spoke of the Holy Spirit, which had not yet been given because He had not yet been glorified. However, when He was glorified, He went to the Father.

Jesus returned to Heaven and sent the Holy Spirit back—why? He said, *"Because if I go, then I will send the Comforter back. Then My Father, the Holy Spirit, and I will abide in you."* (**Jn. 16:7**.)

God lives in us by the Spirit. In Colossians it says, *"For in him dwelleth all the fullness of the Godhead bodily. And ye are complete in him, which is the head of all principality and power:"* (**Col. 2:9-10**.)

Now we have the Father, the Son, and the Holy Ghost, *"all the fullness of the Godhead bodily."* (**Col 2:9**.)

We have received His fullness and now we are complete in Him (see **Col. 2:10**). The Father, the Son, and the Holy Ghost live in us. If the Holy Ghost lives in us, is there ever a time that we do not have the ability? No, because He said we would receive ability and after that, the Holy Ghost would come upon us.

Before, ability was only loaned and then it was taken away, but now ability is resident. Now it is given and it abides.

Jesus, the Last Adam, was restored. Notice what He was doing. Look at all the miracles Jesus did. He turned water into wine. He walked on a stormy sea. He spoke to a fig tree. When you look at everything He did, you will see that He did so many miracles, and they were not just healing. He was basically fixing everything. You must understand that He was operating in the dominion that God gave Adam.

Could Adam have walked on water? Yes, if there had been a storm. For all we know there was no storm before the fall—maybe some wind, who knows; though, no storm. Now, think about that. Adam could have walked on the water. Everything that Jesus was doing He was doing as the Last Adam and He was walking in the dominion that God wanted man to walk. However, man gave it up.

Jesus gave them the authority to become sons, and because they were sons, He sent the spirit of His Son into their hearts crying, "Abba Father." (**Rom 8:15.**)

The Holy Spirit comes upon you, you become a son, and then He sends His Spirit. What happens when you get the Spirit? You get ability, so now you have authority and ability. Plus, you have opportunity to receive manifestations of God's Spirit and ability to see and know things in the unseen spirit realm.

You have the authority of a son to walk in faith and you have the *ability* of the Holy Spirit *(miraculous ability)*, to back it up. Now you have authority and ability.

What does authority and ability equal—dominion? Isn't that simple? Authority and ability equal dominion.

Notice, the way you walk in ability is by accepting responsibility. You must accept responsibility. You can have authority and never use it. You can have ability and never use it. You can have the authority to use the ability but at some point, if you are going to have and walk in ability, you are going to have to accept responsibility.

> You have opportunity to receive manifestations of God's Spirit and ability to see and know things in the unseen spirit realm.

Ability and authority equal dominion and that means that Jesus has put us back into the position that God originally intended, which is to basically look and see this world the way God does. Then we just fix it until it looks the way He wants it to look.

In the book of Matthew, *"Thy Kingdom come. Thy will be done on earth, as it is in heaven."* (**Matt. 6:10.**) Isn't that simple?

Years ago, I heard a story. In Italy, there is a statue of David by Michelangelo. It is an amazing statue. He made many amazing statues, but when he was making the statue of David, someone asked him, "How do you do this?

He was standing there working with a chisel and hammer and this statue was perfect. They asked, "How do you do that? How do you take a block of marble and end up with this?" He said, "It is very simple. I look at what I want to see and then I just chip away everything that does not look like that."

Think about that. That is what God does. He looks at us and as long as we are alive, if we are breathing, everything that does not look like Kingdom can just be chipped away.

When you look at a person, if all you see is what you see, then you are not seeing them through God's eyes. If you look at that person and you see them through God's eyes, you are going to see them on at least two different levels.

If you see a sick person or a crippled person, you see whatever it is on the outside. If you could see them the way God sees them, you would see them the way you would see them in heaven, which means without the wheelchair, without the problem. Your job is just to fix it. You need to see them the way God sees them and then you just chip away everything that does not look like the kingdom.

Chipping away does not have to take years. Chipping away can simply be, "Be healed! Be free!" Whatever it is, you are removing it. You are taking this thing off them and all you are leaving is what God sees.

We talk about physical healing frequently, but let us take it even farther than that for just a second. If you look at a person and all you ever see are their actions, all you are seeing are the results of their thoughts. What you think about, you become. If you think about something long enough or if you talk about it long enough, you will do it.

If you hear a person saying things that do not line up with Scripture, maybe they are lined up with the world. Maybe their actions are their drunkenness, their reveling, and all those kinds of things. The Bible says that if you do those things, then you will not inherit the Kingdom of God.

If that is all you see when you look at that person, and you say, "Oh, look at them. They are drunkards, they are drug addicts, they are doing this or they are doing that," then you know you do not want to have anything to do with them.

I understand that you might not want to fellowship with them. Fellowshipping means that when they raise their glass of alcohol, you raise your hand to alcohol, too.

That is what fellowship means. I can be around them and not fellowship with them. I can be ministering to them, which means that when they raise their glass, I do not have a glass to raise, but I am still ministering to them. In other words, I am not fellowshipping with them, but I can minister to them. I can be around them. They do not defile me because I am holy.

As a matter of fact, if anything, I can sanctify them rather than allow them to defile me because it's not what goes in, but it is what comes out that defiles (see **Matt. 15:11**.)

We should be the salt of this earth. We should be bringing holiness. We should be able to get around people and we should be able to minister to them and talk with them.

Focus On What?

We should not always focus on what they are saying or focus on what they are doing. It takes faith to watch a person get drunk or to watch a person shooting up and yet still see what God sees in them and say, "I know who you can be," without just pushing them aside.

If you are just going to push them aside, all you are going to see is what any human would see. However, if you want to see them through the eyes of God, you are going to have to see them through faith. I am not saying ignore what they are doing. I am saying that you are "mining for precious gold."

Do you understand the analogy there? You are digging for what is deeper than what you can see. I am not saying that the outward thing will not kill them; I am not saying that it will not take them to hell. It easily could. What I am trying to say is that you are going beyond that. You are not overlooking it. You are looking through it and saying, "It is like when they teach princes how to be kings. You are better than this.

You do not know what Jesus died to provide for you." Instead of just looking at what they are doing, looking at what they are saying, and looking at how they are acting.

If that were true, children from two years up to about sixteen or seventeen would just be tossed out—why? It is because they say all kinds of things. They say all kinds of things like, "I hate you! I do not like you."

If you really believed that you would just toss them out on the street, but you are not going to toss a two-year-old out because you look beyond that, and you say, "You do not know what you are saying. I will give you some grace there because you just do not know what you are saying."

We need to be able to do that same thing with people who have bigger problems and to be able to love them into the Kingdom and love the Kingdom into them.

Authority + Power = Dominion. Pray in the spirit to know the will of God, then speak with dominion.

Chapter 9
Dominion Is Not For Wimps

"For whatever is born of God overcomes the world. And this is the victory that has overcome the world—our faith." **(1 Jn. 5:4.)**

There is a huge difference between what we "say" we believe, and what we really believe! There is a very wide gap between our well-spoken prayers in church, and what is discussed in daily conversations. There is a big difference in our theological viewpoints, and the vibrant, conquering church that should be causing the gates of hell to tremble. Our Lord Jesus is still expecting the "church" to influence the world with a bold display of faith that really works!

Christians need to stop whining, complaining, and begging—and come boldly to the throne of grace, asking *The Father's Will* to be done *"on earth as it is in heaven"* (see **Matt 6:10**).

Jesus taught us how to pray—and His kind of praying is expecting and believing for results! The kind of praying that Jesus taught is not simply long, beautiful sounding prayers that just *hope and wish* that something might happen.

Do not "Accept" Everything

Some of us in the 21st century have become so passive (and pathetic), in our faith that we settle for "accepting" every "bad" thing that comes against us by saying: *"Oh well, all things work together for good..."*

That phrase from the eighth chapter of Romans is a very powerful Scripture, especially when used in the context of praying with the help of the mighty Holy Spirit. It was not given to only be used for an excuse for accepting every "bad" thing that comes along. The 'bad' things that come to *steal, kill, and destroy* are from the devil, and should be resisted with the Word of God and prayer (see **Jn. 10:10, Jas. 4:7, 1 Pet. 5:8, and Eph. 6:16.**)

According to the second book of Peter,

> *"Grace and peace be multiplied to you in the knowledge of God and of Jesus our Lord, as His divine power has given to us all things that pertain to life and godliness, through the knowledge of Him who called us by glory and virtue."*
> **2 Pet. 1:2-4**

In this Scripture, it is clear about what "all things" means. It is definitely pertaining to "life and godliness." It does not mean all things in the whole wide world, good things, bad things, sickness, and accidents. This scripture is only referring to things that pertain to "life and godliness."

This is an example of a fundamental rule for interpreting scripture. To understand what a scripture means—it must not be taken out of its context—often taken out of context (see **Rom. 8:28**)!

When you are born again—believing and confessing that Jesus is your Lord and Savior—you are now "in Christ." When you are "in Christ," you have His Word, His authority, and the Holy Spirit to help you overcome the world too!

Spiritually speaking, if we are born again, we are complete in Christ Jesus. We are blessed with every spiritual blessing in heavenly places.

But if we are still "in" our earth clothes—(and must deal with an enemy who is always trying to feed us wrong thinking, condemnation, and discouragement)—we will be fighting the good fight of faith and casting down temptations, complacency, or addictive behavior.

Overcoming Difficult Times

> *"This is the victory that has overcome the world—our faith,"* (1 Jn. 5:4.)

When times get tough, do not be surprised if you feel a heaviness trying to overwhelm you. Do not be surprised if you hear negative thoughts telling you, "It is never going to work out. Things are never going to get better. It is over. It is done."

When those thoughts come, remember, you have a choice—you do not have to believe those lies. You do not have to get on board with negative emotions.

We read in God's Word that King David encountered many difficult situations. That spirit of heaviness tried to steal his destiny. He became depressed and discouraged; though, do you know what he did? He started "talking" to himself. He said, "Why are you cast down, oh my soul? Put your hope in the Lord." He was saying, "David, snap out of it! Why are you discouraged? Why have you lost your joy? God is still on the throne, and He still has good things in store."

When that heaviness tries to come on you, do what David did. Put your trust in the Lord and praise Him—He will give you His strength and empower you to overcome every obstacle you may face!

Your Victory Happens from the Inside Out

You and I will not understand God with our "peewee" brains. We will not understand the purpose of life, what our future is, or why there is so much evil in this world—with our own natural thinking.

God, (and life), is too big to gain understanding that way! God, the Creator, is awesome, perfect, holy, and ultimate truth.

We can only understand God (and the meaning of life), with our spirit—the real you, on the inside! This is why mankind must be "born-again" (on the inside)—so that we can understand spiritual matters of life (see **1 Cor. 2:14.**)

Even then, many people who have had a born-again Christian experience still use their own natural reasoning to navigate through life.

Do not feel bad, because most religious scholars, scientists, and professors are trying to understand God's Word with their own natural (peewee) thinking too!

> *"The natural man does not receive the things of the spirit of God, for they are foolishness to him; nor can he know them, because they are spiritually discerned."* (**1 Cor. 2:14.**)

With your "aggressive" and pro-active shield of faith—you will "let it bounce" when you feel like giving up, or when negative emotions try to dominate your thinking.

The Church Is Supernatural

The church of the Lord Jesus Christ is a supernatural entity. When you remove the supernatural power of God from the church, you do not have a church anymore; you merely have a religious organization.

In the first book of the New Testament, Matthew, Jesus described the church, *"And I say also to you, that you are Peter, and upon this rock I will build My church; and the gates of hell shall not prevail against it."* (**Matt. 16:18.**)

The Greek word translated "church," *ekklesia*, means "an assembly of called out ones." The church worldwide is the collective gathering of God's people. This gathering is Christ's church. Moreover, Christ is the Anointed One. Therefore, the church is the anointed, dynamic, yoke-destroying, burden-removing, supernatural power of God.

What Will You Call It?

The first book of Corinthians instructs us, *"Pursue love, and desire spiritual gifts, but especially that you may prophesy."* (**1 Cor. 14:1-2.**)

As we consider what the Lord has gifted us, we will discover that He also wants us to decree, prophesy, declare, profess, and speak to mountains of problems (see **Job 22:28** and **Matt. 21**).

We should also consider how the Lord God created us, *"Let Us make man in Our image, according to Our likeness..."* (**Gen. 1:26.**) Indeed, we are to be *"imitators of God as dear children."* (**Eph. 5:1.**)

As children of God we can speak like God, *"who gives life to the dead and 'calls' those things which do not exist as though they did,"* (**Rom. 4:17-b**).

During a conversation or email, take an opportunity to Prophesy:

* I call you blessed.

* I call you anointed.

* I call your family restored.

* I call your family set-free.

* I call you prosperous.

* I call you a child of God.

* I call you healed.

* I call you faith filled.

* I call you Spirit-led.

* I call you an overcomer.

* I call you a conqueror!

* I call you a mountain mover!

The phrase, *"and calleth those things which be not as though they were,"* is referring to the instance Paul had just cited when God changed Abram's name to Abraham (see **Gen. 17:5**). According to Strong's Concordance, the name Abram means "high father," and the name Abraham means "father of a multitude."

The Lord changed Abram's name to Abraham one year before the birth of Isaac, thus confessing that Abraham was the father of a multitude before it happened in the physical. This illustrates God's faith. God says things are so before there is physical proof that they are so. The same thing was done at creation (see **Gen. 1**). God spoke everything into existence, and then it was so. He spoke light into existence and then four days later created a source for that light to come from (see **Gen. 1:3** and **Gen. 1:14-19**).

God has given us the power to create with faith-filled words (see **Prov. 18:20-21, Mk. 11:14, 23**). If we are going to operate in God's kind of faith, we must learn to call those things that are not as though they were.

Abraham Considered Not

The book of Romans tells us about faith:

> *"And not being weak in faith, he did not consider his own body, already dead (since he was about a hundred years old), and the deadness of Sarah's womb. He did not waver at the promise of God through unbelief, but was strengthened in faith, giving glory to God."* **Rom. 4:19-20**

The word "consider" is defined as "**1.** To think carefully about. **2.** To regard as. **3.** To take into account" (American Heritage Dictionary). The Greek word that was used here for "consider" is *katanoeo*, and it simply means "to observe fully" (Strong's Concordance).

Therefore, we can see that Abraham did not think carefully about his age, and Sarah's, and the impact that it would have on the promise that God had given him. He did not consider those things or make any allowance for them. That was not what he paid attention to.

That is amazing, and that is exactly the reason many of us would not be able to receive the same miracle.

We consider every negative thing that looks contrary to God's promises, and then we try to use our faith to overcome the fear and unbelief that come with those thoughts, (see **Matt. 17:20**). That is not the way Abraham was strong in faith.

1 Corinthians tells us about things that are not:

> *"God has chosen the foolish things of the world to put to shame the wise, and God has chosen the weak things of the world to put to shame the things which are mighty; and the base things of the world and the things which are despised God has chosen, and the things which are not, to bring to nothing the things that are."* **1 Cor. 1:27-28**

In the book of Ezekiel, there is an instruction from the Lord: He said to Ezekiel, *"Prophesy to these bones, and say to them, 'O dry bones, hear the word of the LORD!'"* (**Ezek. 37:4.**)

In the book of the Acts of the Apostles, John and Peter 'called', a crippled man healed: *"In the name of Jesus Christ of Nazareth, rise up and walk."* (**Acts 3:1-4.**)

If you are tempted to gossip, complain, or whine, do not give in to the devil's snare. Raise your *shield of faith* and "Let it bounce!"

Chapter 10
Dominion and Authority

> *"Christ has redeemed us from the curse of the law, having become a curse for us (for it is written, "Cursed is everyone who hangs on a tree"), that the blessing of Abraham might come upon the Gentiles in Christ Jesus, that we might receive the promise of the Spirit through faith."* **Gal. 3:13-14**

Spiritual dominion and authority are God's gift to all believers! If it is true that God has granted believers dominion and authority on earth—and that we have been redeemed from the curse of sin, sickness, poverty, fear, and demonic oppression—then why is the church of Jesus the Christ in such bad shape?

We should be mountain movers, laying hands on the sick, and casting out devils!

It is because we have been taught wrong in many churches. We have been taught a bunch of religious excuses, instead of the pure Word of God and the power of the Holy Spirit.

Jesus made the promise to give us dominion and authority in the book of Matthew when he said to Peter: *"The gates of Hades will not be able to withstand or withhold the advancing church."* (**Matt. 16:18.**) Jesus was going to build His church. The church was going to advance. The gates of Hades could not withstand it.

Jesus is saying that He who is in us is greater than he who is in the world. (**1 Jn. 4:4.**) His power is greater than the power of the enemy. When there is a head-on conflict between the power of the enemy and the power of God, the power of the enemy will lose every time.

How do we then live and walk in this dominion and authority? We understand that the world we live in has two realms—the natural and the spiritual. We need to be able to know how to live in this spiritual realm in a way that affects the natural realm.

As I read Paul's amazing statement in the first book to the Corinthians, I begin to understand the power we have as believers. Paul says in these verses that he's coming to Corinth to see the teachers that are there, and he's not coming to hear their words, but he's coming to see the power in their lives, *"for the kingdom of God is not words, but it is power."* (**1 Cor. 4:19-20.**)

Christ's Power and Dominion

Paul says to the Ephesians, *"I pray that you'll begin to understand the incredible greatness of his power."* (**Eph. 1:19.**) Now just prior to this Paul said, *"I pray that a spirit of wisdom and revelation will be given to you,"* and he was praying that it would happen in three areas. One of the areas had to do with the power of God. Paul says:

> *"I pray that your hearts will be flooded with light so that you can understand the confident hope he has given to those he called—his holy people who are his rich and glorious inheritance. I also pray that you will understand the incredible greatness of God's power for us who believe him. This is the same mighty power."* **Eph. 1:18-19, NLT**

In between Christ's resurrection and ascension, he exhorted his disciples several times about his commission for them to go through Jerusalem, Judea, Samaria, and the outermost parts of the earth. He told them not to try to embark on this mission until first being clothed with power from on high, from God. Therefore, the disciples waited in the upper room, where God's Spirit was released upon them.

In the Gospels, Jesus models for his church what he wants us to do and be, including living in God's power. When I read the Gospels, I am seeing the CEO of the church, the head of the church, not just telling us what to do, but *modeling* for us what he wants us to do. It is a challenge for us as believers in westernized Christianity to look at the life and ministry of Jesus and see how our church is measuring up. The church of Jesus Christ is to be carrying on the ministry that Jesus began in the Gospels. That is why he says, *"As the Father sent me into the world, I'm now sending you."* (**Jn. 17:18**.) That was the last night, the end of his earthly ministry. He is saying I am now sending you out the same way the Father sent me.

The Early Church

In the book of Acts, the early church is living out the life of the ministry of Jesus Christ without the incarnate Jesus. In other words, it can be done with Jesus ascended. He sent the Holy Spirit to be the Comforter and the one by whom we would carry out life and ministry.

From Romans through the end of the New Testament, there are truths, theology, and doctrine that demonstrate why and how we can live like Jesus and like the early church in the Book of Acts. When Jesus was living and ministering on earth, he was living and ministering as true man. Jesus as true God became true man. In that unique personage, he is both God and man. When he was ministering on earth, though, he was ministering in the capacity as man without falling back as a safety net on his attributes as God. He was showing us what a human being living in the right relationship with God could live like.

So that gives us a backdrop as we come into Ephesians (see **Eph. 1**). How is it that we can live the life that Jesus lived? Paul says in, *"I pray that you'll gain insight and understanding. I pray that you'll get revelation* *into the surpassing greatness of the power of God that's at work in you."* (**Eph. 1:17.**)

Later in the same chapter from the book of Ephesians, Paul says that the power at work in you is the very power that raised Jesus Christ from death. How many of us have ever thought of our bodies being vessels that carry the power of God, the very power that raised Jesus Christ from death? Let us say this aloud together: "The power that raised Jesus from death is resident in me." (See **Rom 8:11**.)

Release of the power You Have

How many of us need revelation to understand what it truly means? How many of us ask, "Do I need more power?" What hinders us from a life of God's power is not the need to get more power, but instead it is that we need a release of the power we have already been given in our union with Jesus Christ through salvation.

For that reason, what is inhibiting it from being released in my life? We cannot minister in God's authority when we are not living under God's authority. Jesus Christ, as true God yet true man, lived underneath the Father's authority—Jesus said that there was nothing he said or did that he had not first heard from the Father. In other words, Jesus lived under the authority of his heavenly Father.

Here are a couple verses that show that: *"But I do nothing without consulting the Father. I do just as I am told. My judgment is absolutely just because it is according to the will of God, who sent me. It's not merely my own."* (**Jn. 5:30.**)

> *"I have much to say about you and much to condemn, but I won't, for I say only what I have heard from the one who sent me, and he is true."* So Jesus said, *"When you have lifted up the Son of Man on the cross, then you will realize that I am he and that I do nothing on my own, but I speak what the Father taught me."* **Jn. 8:26, 28**

Jesus only did what he saw and heard from the Father.

The reason Jesus' power is released and available so much more in the Gospels than it is for us is that Jesus was sensitive to make sure that everything he did and said was in obedience to the Father. He lived in the will of God. He did not have a spirit of independence, rebellion, or insurrection. He had a spirit of submission to the Father.

Each of us should ask: Do I have any independence in my life? Do I have any lack of submission? Do I have any rebellion? Jesus understood how important it is that he did not allow rebellion to be in his life. The first book of Samuel says, *"rebellion is as the sin of … witchcraft."* (**1 Sam. 15:23.**) Jesus ministered under God's authority. We must be sensitive that we are living in proper relationship and alignment with God's authority.

As the Father sent the Son into the world, the Son sends us in the world (see **Jn. 17:18**). If I am on Earth with the mission of the Father to do the works Jesus did, then I will because Jesus made a promise that not only will I do the very works that He did, but also I will do greater works than He did (see **Jn. 14:12**). The church of Jesus Christ in westernized Christianity is not normal. We must redefine normal. What is normal for the church of Jesus Christ? It is the Gospels. It is the Book of Acts and doing what Jesus did and even greater things than He did. The church is to be about making statements about the kingdom of God.

After Jesus sets captives free and heals diseases, and the gospel is presented clearly, Jesus said the kingdom of God is here. For me to do the ministry of Jesus, I am going to need a power that is greater than what I possess in and of myself. God knew that, and that is why God gave it to us. I have his power right here, right now. It has settled, sealed, done, and complete. I have the very power that raised Jesus Christ from the dead.

The Difference Between Power and Authority

There is a difference between authority and power. A distinction between power and authority is shown in the Gospel of Luke: *"All the people were amazed and said to each other, 'What is this teaching? With authority and power he gives orders to evil spirits, and they come out.'"* (**Lk. 4:36.**) Luke goes on to say, *"He called the twelve together and gave them power and authority over all the demons and to heal all diseases."* (**Lk. 9:1.**)

Although, we find another clue that the disciples were in unbelief—probably because of seeing the seizures, (see **Matt. 17:19-21**).

Authority is the capacity we have due to our *position in Christ*. I have the authority of God "in me" due to my union with Christ Jesus.

We receive power when the Holy Spirit comes "upon" us, (see **Acts 1:8**). Power is the capacity and spiritual strength I have due to my life *posture in Christ*. For instance, Jesus said in the beginning of **Luke 9** He had given his authority and power to the twelve, and they went out and did amazing miraculous signs and wonders (see **Luke 9**). A little bit farther in the same chapter from the book of Luke, Jesus is on the Mount of Transfiguration with Peter, James, and John. A man comes to his other disciples down below and says, "Will you heal my son, for he is caught up in these seizures by demonic activity?" They were not able to heal him. When Jesus comes down off the Mount of Transfiguration, the man comes up to him and says, "I asked your disciples if they would heal my son, and they could not. Will you?" Jesus then heals the son.

> Power is the capacity and spiritual strength I have due to my life posture in Christ.

Was it God's will for the son to be healed? Yes. Had the disciples received authority to do that? Yes. Why was the power not released for it to happen? Well, that was the question the disciples had. They asked, "Jesus, why were we not able to heal him?" In addition, Jesus says, *"This kind comes out by prayer and fasting."* Actually, 'this kind' was their 'unbelief', (see **Matt. 17:19-21**), would come out by prayer and fasting.

Now I do not know all that was meant in Jesus' response to that, but here is what I believe it means. I believe Jesus was saying, "You guys were depending only on yourself. Where was the prayer? Where was the sense of your dependence on the Holy Spirit?"

Ongoing prayer in the Holy Spirit in preparation for ministry is certainly needed, but I just wonder if it is not possible that they may have been relying on their own capacity, and nothing happened. Sometimes strongholds—places where the enemy has a base of operation, such as pride—makes the release of the authority of God less important. God resists the proud, but he gives grace to the humble.

Rebellion will also reduce the power of God to a lower level of importance to us. Nevertheless, the power that raised Jesus from death should be primarily in our lives.

Fear has the same effect. At Kadesh-Barnea, when the Israelites had the option of going into the Promised Land, they heard about the giants and in fear said no, and then judgment came. God called them an evil generation because of their fear. Sometimes we look at fear as being unfortunate, while God calls it evil and wicked.

Subsequently, I must change my perception of what may seem to us to be harmless issues, which in reality are very important issues if God's authority and power are going to be released in my life. Remember, when Jesus was in Nazareth, Scripture says he could not perform miracles there because of their lack of faith (see **Mk. 6:5-6**). Unbelief can compromise the release of God's power in me.

Power is Relative

Authority is an absolute that we have in Christ, but power is relative. It is related to our life being submitted to the Holy Spirit. That is why my being set free, my restoration, and living free is more than just about me. It is about others that I will minister to. It is about the lives that God wants me to be used in. It is about seeing the kingdom of God advancing so the gates of Hades cannot withstand it. When there is an encounter between the kingdom of darkness and the kingdom of light, the kingdom of light will win every time.

To this extent, the kingdom of darkness must try to compromise the power of God in me through fear, unbelief, rebellion, and other sinful thoughts and emotions.

Therefore, I want to align my life to release power and authority. There is a difference between striving and aligning. By aligning, I mean bringing myself in alignment with God's truth. I want to bring my life into greater and greater alignment with God and His truth so His power can be released in my life in an increased measure. He has given me the power that raised Jesus from death (see **Rom. 8:11**). He has given me the Holy Spirit. With all that he has given me for spiritual weapons and resources, I have all I need for life and godliness (see **2 Pet. 1:3**). I just need to start operating it.

> I want to bring my life into greater and greater alignment with God and his truth so His power can be released in my life in an increased measure.

What would it be like to see every believer, every marriage, every family, and every church that names the name of Christ moving operational in the authority in Jesus' name and yielding to the power of the Holy Spirit? Hell could not withstand it (see **Matt. 16:18**). Thusly, the renewal, rejuvenation, and reformation of the church are crucial to God's kingdom mission.

Power is relative to being submitted to the Holy Spirit.

Chapter 11
Dominion of Kings and Priests

"And have made us kings and priests to our God; and we shall reign on the earth." (**Rev. 5:10**)

I am destined to be a king and a priest. Really? As I look in the mirror, it seems ridiculous and unreal. But the reality is that God Himself performed a miracle inside me and inside you. After we declare and confess Jesus as Savior, (see **Rom. 10:9**,) and that Jesus was raised from the dead—we have been born from above (see **Eph. 2:1**).

Obviously, this inner transformation is not our own doing! It was Jesus who *"has made us kings and priests to His God and Father, to Him be glory and dominion forever and ever. Amen."* (**Rev 1:5-6.**)

Throughout Scripture, it is abundantly clear that miracles are part of God's plan. We see God's hand for interrupting the natural course of the human experience with miraculous displays of His power. By giving believers dominion on the earth, God is continuing His plan for power and miracles through us.

> By giving believers dominion on the earth, God is continuing His plan for power and miracles through us.

God's original intention for mankind is to expand His kingdom on earth. God's will has always been that His people should fulfill the two ministries of king and priest.

Exodus 19:5-6 prophesied,

> *"Now therefore, if you will indeed obey my voice and keep My covenant, then you shall be a special treasure to Me above all peoples; for all the earth is mine. And you will be to Me a kingdom of priests and a holy nation."* **Ex. 19:5-16**

Living like Kings

When we become a new creation in Christ (see **2 Cor. 5:17**), God has, *"delivered us from the power of darkness and conveyed us into the kingdom of the Son of His love."* (**Col. 1:13.**) Nevertheless, we still have a big choice to make. Will we live as a slave under condemnation of the enemy, or as a king and priest under Christ Jesus? The choice is easy. We are God's representatives, called to bring heaven to earth wherever we go.

The First Epistle of Peter describes our position like this,

> *"you are a chosen generation, a royal priesthood, a holy nation, His own special people, that you may proclaim the praises of Him who called you out of darkness into His marvelous light."* **1 Pet. 2:9**

I like to review the Amplified version of the Scriptures from the book of Romans:

> *"For if because of one man's trespass (lapse, offense) death reigned through that one, much more surely will those who receive [God's] overflowing grace (unmerited favor) and the free gift of righteousness [putting them into right standing with Himself] reign as kings in life through the one Man Jesus Christ (the Messiah, the Anointed One)."* **Rom. 5:17**

Dominion of Kings and Priests

Some people might recall a scripture that says, *"don't think of yourself more highly than you ought."* (**Rom. 12:3**.) In the natural, we should not think of our carnal (sense-realm) self too highly. However, as Romans instructs us we renew our minds and prove the will of God and how He sees us (see **Rom. 12:2**). Moreover, God sees us as He created us in our spirit as kings and priests.

God Made Us Kings and Priests

The first book of Peter tells us we belong to, *"a royal priesthood."* (**1 Pet. 2:9**.) The word *royal* speaks of our kingly attributes as believers. A king has the legal power to make decrees. He legislates, he conforms, he summons, he authorizes,—that is what a king does! A king does not beg and cry for anything. He declares something and that thing is established.

> The whole universe is waiting for us to give it instruction.

Remember, Jesus is King of kings. He is the capital "K" King, and we are the lowercase "k" kings. Believers are destined to manifest our royal anointing to decree blessings over our marriage, family, business, ministry, and every other realm in our sphere of influence.

The whole universe is waiting for us to give it instruction. The scripture says, *"For the earnest expectation of creation eagerly waits for the revealing of the sons of God."* (**Rom. 8:19**.)

Believer's Role as a Priest

Both the Old and New Testaments describe a priest as one who offers sacrifices. Believers who rule and demonstrate dominion on earth will learn to serve as priests of almighty God.

Here are some specific responsibilities of those called to act as priests in God's kingdom:

1. Present our bodies as a living sacrifice.

Romans instructs, *"I beseech you therefore, brethren, by the mercies of God, that you present your bodies a living sacrifice, holy, acceptable to God, which is your reasonable service."* (**Rom. 12:1.**)

This sacrifice is our reasonable service, given of our own free will.

2. Sacrifices of praise and worship.

Hebrews instructs, *"Therefore by Him let us continually offer the sacrifice of praise to God, that is, the fruit of our lips, giving thanks to His name."* (**Heb. 13:15.**)

To always praise God, regardless of the circumstances or how we feel, is one of the most important sacrifices a believer can offer.

3. Offer physical gifts to God.

The high priest under the law of Moses presented both gifts and sacrifices to God on behalf of the people (see **Heb. 5:1**). Similarly, Jesus, as our High Priest, receives our tithes and offerings and presents them to God (see **Heb 7:8**).

Believer's Role as a King

In our role as kings in God's kingdom, we have the legal authority to act as God acts in heaven and to carry out His will through the power of the Holy Spirit.

Under a full monarchy, when a king makes a decree, a proclamation, or a declaration—it becomes law. We are God's kings and priests (see **Rev. 1:6; Rev. 5:10**), and when we make declarations in line with His will, spiritually speaking, they have "legal" authority in the spiritual realm. "Authority" is the legal right to exercise power and "power" is the ability to do something.

Let us explore further about our kingly role under Christ:

1. Rule with the Rod of Authority

The Psalms' prophesy, *"The Lord said to my Lord, Sit at My right hand, till I make Your enemies Your footstool."* (**Ps. 110:1.**)

Christ sat down at the right hand of the Father because His work was completely done. His sacrifice was eternal, and the victory He achieved was irrevocable.

Psalms goes on to say, *"The Lord shall send the rod of Your strength out of Zion. Rule in the midst of Your enemies! Your people shall be volunteers in the day of Your power."* (**Ps. 110:2-3.**)

The rod, in older times, represents the king's authority—in the case of the above scripture, the authority of King Jesus. After Jesus resurrected, ascended, and sat on His throne, He gave us authority to use His "rod" over nations and to expand His kingdom. In other words, believers now have the assignment to carry out the Father God's plans and purposes (see **Matt 28:18-20**).

2. Rule Through Prayer

Ruling through prayer is one way in which the roles of king and priest overlap. In God's unseen kingdom, presidents, prime ministers, dictators, senators, congressmen, and so forth do not rule the world. These leaders rule in the natural, physical realm. However, those who know how to pray and rule to establish the kingdom of God activate true power in the spirit realm.

We will be able to rule through prayer when we meet the following conditions:

* Our prayers must be based on scripture.

God's will is His Word. When we pray according to God's Word, He hears us (see **1 Jn. 5:14**).

* Our prayers must correspond to the *rhema* of God.

Rhema is the divine *anointed, spoken* Word of God. The Greek word *logos* is often used to describe the written Word of God, while the Greek word rhema is applied to a word that is a received by *divine, anointed revelation*. The Holy Spirit gives a rhema word for a specific moment and situation—often resulting in supernatural manifestations.

* Our prayers must be empowered by the Holy Spirit.

God's Word and the Holy Spirit always work together. The Holy Spirit will empower our prayers only when they align with the Word.

You Are God's Special People

The apostle Peter prophesied the purpose of all believers,

> *"You are a chosen generation, a royal priesthood, a holy nation, His own special people, that you may proclaim the praises of Him who called you out of darkness into His marvelous light."* **1 Pet. 2:9**

Jesus died for this very purpose. By His blood, He cleansed, justified, and redeemed us to make us kings and priests with power to continue His ministry on earth.

Eagles are known for their strength, boldness, keenness of vision, and gracefulness. Believers should be known for spiritual strength, boldness, faith-filled vision, and grace.

Chapter 12
Called to Conquer

"In all these things we are more than conquerors through Him that loves us." (**Rom. 8:37**)

As believers in Christ, we are called not only to walk in authority and freedom, but also to conquer our enemy. The enemy is not physical or fleshly, but spiritual.

To conquer is to overcome and take control by force. The word conquer implies the image of a powerful army seizing back control of a fortress or another type of military outpost.

It is time to take control of your mind. It is time to take back control of your life. This is not a passive action; it requires spiritual force!

God does not want you and me to coexist with the *powers of darkness*—He wants you to *conquer* them.

The scriptures declare that we are "more than conquerors" through Him who loves us (see **Rom. 8:37**). This term *more than conquerors* are derived from the Greek compound word *hupernikao*, which means, "to vanquish…gain a surpassing victory!

In other words, God does not want us to merely survive; or just *get through* the works of Satan. He wants us to experience a surpassing victory over the enemy of our souls. This victory is possible because Jesus has already conquered the devil!

We believers must realize the magnitude of the power within you through the finished works of Jesus at the Cross, the whipping post, and the resurrection. You are supernaturally powerful (see **Acts 1:8**). You are mighty in the Lord (see **Eph. 6:10-11**). You are in Christ and Christ is in you (see **2 Cor. 5:17**).

Take It by Force

> *"And from the days of John the Baptist until now the kingdom of heaven suffers violence, and the violent take it by force."* (**Matt. 11:12**.)

We have been called to conquer the enemy's kingdom and to seize our freedom by force. Whatever demonic oppression you refuse to drive out of your life will ultimately drive you out of the path of God's blessings and promises for your life (see **Num. 33:52-53**).

The word violence in Matthew comes from the Greek word *biazo*—to use force (see **Matt. 11:12**). I believe this scripture is related to the imprisonment and murder of John the Baptist. (I believe this event was the imprisoned, soon to be murdered, Baptist's inquiry concerning Christ that promoted what seems best read as a negative evaluation of John/Christ's opponents and their agenda.) Therefore, I believe the word *force* can defined as "strength or energy as an attribute of physical action or movement. In other words, force is *power in action*.

How do we act against the enemy? The basis for all **spiritual** power is revelation. After the Holy Spirit has revealed God's Word to us, and we act upon that revelation, it releases supernatural power that brings freedom, healing, and deliverance in our lives. We also enforce spiritual power through the spoken Word of God.

If the devil is oppressing you in any way, do not remain silent; open your mouth and declare God's Word. Remember, *"they overcame him (Satan) by the blood of the Lamb and the word of their testimony"* (**Rev 12:11**).

Reign in Life as a King

We have been 'made' conquerors through our Lord Jesus. The apostle Paul said it like this: *"For if by the one man's offense death reigned through the one, much more those who receive abundance of grace and of the gift of righteousness will reign in life through the One, Jesus Christ."* (**Rom. 5:17.**) The Amplified version of this verse says, *"...reign in life as a king." (***Rom. 5:17, AMP***)*

The "death" spoken of in the first part of this verse is not limited to physical death. It includes that, but the wage of sin is death (see **Rom 6:23**).

Anything that comes because of sin is death. Shame is death. Sickness, poverty, divorce, war, and all things that came because of the 'Fall' are death.

There are many in the modern-day church who will say their sins are forgiven, but they do not believe they are righteous. Yet this verse and its context are saying this gift was not just salvation, forgiveness of sins (see **Eph. 1:7**), but right standing, or righteousness, with God as a gift. This is foreign to many Christians, but it is the foundation of grace reigning in our lives (see **Rom. 5:21**).

Notice that we must receive the abundance of God's grace AND the gift of righteousness to reign in life. Receiving grace is essential, but it will not result in us reigning until we couple it with our right standing in Christ and all the privileges that come with that.

More Than Conquerors

How can we be more than conquerors? Conquerors have the victory and the spoils of war, but they must fight to get them. We are more than conquerors because we have victory and all the spoils of war, but we did not do the fighting. Jesus fought and won this battle for us, and all we must do is receive the benefits. That is being more than conquerors.

New Testament Believers

It is vitally important to understand the huge difference between the Old Testament and the New Testament. Almost every born-again Christian will know that the cross is the dividing line between the two. Although, the practical everyday application of God's promises loses its strength, when the awesome grace of God is combined with the laws of Moses.

The good news of the gospel is a demonstration of the freedom we have in Christ as 'fulfilling' the rigid requirements of Old Testament sacrifices and works. Jesus said, *"Do not think that I came to destroy the Law or the Prophets. I did not come to destroy but to fulfill."*

Along with the wonderful grace, New Testament believers enjoy—every individual also can live with the supernatural power of the mighty Holy Spirit.

Why Be Strong to Conquer

One thing has become very clear. Satan has declared all-out war on our families, children, cities, nations, and every institution on Earth. The whole Earth is shaking and trembling under the assault of the kingdom of darkness. Still, at the same time, I can sense a remnant of believers beginning to arise with a dominion attitude against spiritual wickedness.

It has been a long time since the kingdom of darkness has had to deal with believers who realize their identity, dominion, and inheritance in Christ.

The wars that need fighting are the ones we start by going forward after principalities and every high thing that exalts itself against the Kingdom of God. A passive church, as most have been, will not win this spiritual war. It is time that we put on the full nature of Christ (see **Eph. 4:13-14**.) and vanquish the works of Satan. *"For this purpose the*

Son of God was manifested, that He might destroy the works of the devil," (**1 Jn. 3:8.**)

Revelation Knowledge

There is natural knowledge, but then there is knowledge that comes from the inside out of your spirit, not your brain. You can have knowledge of some great Bible promises and believe them, but until you have revelation knowledge about Romans, it will be tough to live your life with the supernatural power that God has given us to reign in life as a king (see **Rom. 5:17**)!

A lack of revelation knowledge is the greatest cause of faith failures.

Most Christians believe the Word of God with their brains, but they have not meditated on it enough for it to "light up" in their hearts. If they had, that Word would absolutely revolutionize their lives. Nothing would be able to shake them loose from it.

In the kingdom of God, there is a knowing that comes from the inside out, rather than the outside in. It comes directly from God to our spirit.

The best description of revelation knowledge was when Jesus asked His disciples who they thought He was.

Jesus had asked the disciples, *"Who do you say I am?"* Peter answered Him by declaring, *"You are the Christ, the Son of the living God."* (**Matt. 16:16.**) *"Blessed are you, Simon…"* Jesus responded, *"because flesh and blood has not revealed this to you, but My Father who is in heaven."* (**Matt. 16:17, NASB.**)

Do not Dishonor the Lord

Do people dishonor the lord? Yes! In fact, some Christians do the same thing when they resist some of the finished works Jesus did at the whipping post, the cross, in the belly of the Earth, the resurrection, and the ascension back to heaven.

How do some resist the finished works of Jesus? They dishonor the Lord, when they resist the very things that Jesus shed His blood to give us—what things? Healing for all, salvation for all, baptism with the Holy Spirit (see **Acts 2:4**), gifts of the Spirit (see **1 Cor. 12**), and speaking with other tongues (**1 Cor 14**).

Do not Blame God

This is also dishonoring the Lord when preachers say to the Lord's sheep that 'everything that happens is the will of God.' Think about it! In the earth today, there is much sin, lots of murders, stealing, and wars, selling of drugs, slavery, poverty, and the deceitfulness of riches. None of these things are the will of God.

You will experience as much of God's power as you can believe and receive.

Chapter 13
YOUR POSITION OF POWER

"raised us up together, and made us sit together in the heavenly places in Christ Jesus." (**Eph. 2:6**)

Why so many believers are bound and held captive by the enemy? The answer is found, in general, in the fact that many have neglected a vital component of spiritual authority. Instead of feeding their spirit with an uncompromised Word of God, many believers listen to Christian leaders who are feeding them with religious tradition and excuses. (**Mk. 7:13**.)

Take Your Seat and Be Complete

What believers need to learn is that they have been given a powerful position as a "new creation" in Christ (see **2 Cor. 5:17**). This position is possible because of the "finished work" of Chris after His resurrection and ascension. The statement, "sit together in heavenly places" (see **Eph. 2:6**.) is one of the most powerful statements in all the scriptures! This statement firmly establishes the church, (the body of Christ), with authority in heaven and in Earth (see **Eph. 1:22**).

Remember, God delegated dominion to Adam over the Earth. Now, after the resurrection and ascension of Jesus—all authority (and dominion) was given to Jesus, over both heaven and Earth—and by supernatural association to the body of Christ—the church. This was a total shock to

Satan and his principalities and powers—because now Jesus was seated at the right hand of the Father God. Additionally, a double shock: every believer is raised up to be seated with Christ! However, just because believers have all authority, which does not mean that, we automatically have victory. Why? Because Satan is an outlaw! He did not respect God's position, so he will not respect your position authority either.

Spiritual War

The book of Ephesians tells us that we are in a spiritual battle with renegade spirits, and we must enforce our spiritual authority over principalities and powers (see **Eph. 6:10-18**). Our victories are won by forcing demonic spirits to submit to the Word of God.

Our assignment as the church is to control and patrol the heavenly places. When we control the heavenly places, the Earth will line up!

We will operate in authority and dominion when we submit to God's Word as final authority; regardless of what naysayers may teach (see **Jas. 4:7**).

A Centurion Knows Authority

A centurion related his confidence in Jesus' authority to heal when he said, *"For I am a man under authority ..."* (**Matt. 8:9**). The centurion expressed his understanding of the power of authority. He knew that a person with authority needs only to speak the word, and whatever he has ordered will happen. Now remember, Jesus gave us His authority when He said, *"I give you authority ..."* (**Lk. 10:19**). Jesus also gave authority to believers as we read, (see **Lk. 9:1, 10:1, Mk. 11:23, 16:17-18**). All authority is transferred from one person to another.

When you operate as a rogue agent, you really have no authority at all. Millions of Christians have no regard for the spiritual authority of godly leaders in the body of Christ. They are not submitted to any pastor or spiritual leader. This makes them unfamiliar with how biblical authority works, and this makes them vulnerable to the oppression of the devil (see **Heb. 13:16-18**).

If you want to win spiritual battles, you must learn to come under godly authority. Even Satan's kingdom is highly organized (see **Eph. 6:12-13**). Like the centurion, we are under the authority of Jesus, and we can use authority and dominion to win spiritual battles (see **Matt. 8**).

God's Kingdom Revealed

The more we understand the kingdom of God, the more we will understand dominion and authority, and the more we will be in *position* to resist and dominate the works of the devil.

In the Gospel of Matthew Jesus said, *"lead us not into temptation, but deliver us from evil; for Yours is the kingdom, and the power, and the glory, forever."* (**Matt. 6:13**.)

The "kingdom," as used in Matthew, is derived from the Greek word *basileia*, which refers to royal power, dominion, and rule (see **Matt. 6:13**). It is the right to rule over or govern a kingdom. Simply put, the kingdom of God is the government and rule of God in heaven and on earth.

As citizens of God's kingdom, we have been granted the power to rule and reign on the earth. Our ultimate rule and reign will come at the end of this age when we reign with Christ at His second coming (see **2 Tim. 2:12; Rev. 20:6**). God has also given us the right to have dominion and reign in the spiritual realm *here and now*! (**1 Jn. 4:17**.)

We exercise our spiritual kingship by taking dominion over the forces of darkness (demonic spirits, sickness, and oppression).

A Better Revelation of 'All Things' in Christ

Our position includes promoting the truth about Christ to the world. In other words, we have good news to share, and this news is 'truth' according to the Word of God.

According to the Second Epistle of Peter,

> *"Grace and peace be multiplied to you in the knowledge of God and of Jesus our Lord, as His divine power has given to us **all things** that pertain to life and godliness, through the knowledge of Him who called us by glory and virtue."* **2 Pet. 1:2-4**

In this scripture, it is clear about what "all things" means. It is definitely pertaining to "life and godliness." It **does not** mean all things in the whole wide world, good things, bad things, sickness, and accidents. This scripture is only referring to things that pertain to "life and godliness."

This is an example of a fundamental rule for interpreting scripture. To understand what a scripture means it must not be taken out of its context.

Unfortunately, many scriptures are taken out of their context—and given an erroneous meaning.

A good example of a scripture that is taken out of context is, *"And we know that **all things** work together for good to those who love God, to those who are the called according to His purpose."* (**Rom. 8:28.**)

The word "and" should give anyone a clue that continues from the previous scriptures that are all about how the Holy Spirit helps us in intercession (prayer) (see **Rom. 8:28**). Many good Christians have taken this scripture out of context—and teach that all things include all things in the whole world; good, bad, sickness, and accidents. Not true! The verse is only referring to all things in prayer will work together for good.

To understand what a scripture means it must not be taken out of its context.

Here is another scripture that can be misinterpreted, *"Therefore, if anyone is in Christ, he is a new creation; old things have passed away; behold, **all things** have become new."* (**2 Cor. 5:17**)

This scripture is an easy one to understand. In addition, most teachers will leave it in the context of pertaining to the new creation. All things here is only referring to your born-again spirit. In other words, it is referring to "life and godliness" in your spirit, not your body or mind.

Here is another scripture that can be misinterpreted, *"I can do all things through Christ who strengthens me."* (**Phil. 4:13.**)

This scripture is also an easy one to understand. Furthermore, most teachers will leave it in context. All things here are only referring to "life and godliness." In other words, it does not refer to doing ungodly things.

Here is another scripture that can be easily interpreted, *"But seek first the kingdom of God and His righteousness, and **all these things** shall be added to you."* (**Matt. 6:33.**)

This scripture demonstrates how some verses refer to all **these** things as listed.

Basically, whenever a scripture refers to "all things" it is pertaining to "life and godliness" and the subject "in context."

Another scripture that is often taken out of context, *"giving **thanks** always for **all things** to God the Father in the name of our Lord Jesus Christ."* (**Eph. 5:20.**)

In context, this verse follows being filled with the Spirit—and speaking to one another in psalms and hymns and spiritual songs, singing, and making melody in your heart to the Lord.

We are not instructed to give thanks for all things in the whole world; good, bad, sickness, and accidents.

We give thanks for all things pertaining to being filled with the Spirit.

Another scripture that emphasizes the "all things" example is, *"All things are lawful for me, but not all things are helpful; all things are lawful for me, but not all things edify."* (**1 Cor. 10:23.**)

In other words, God's Word, especially in the 'new' covenant, always promotes godly instruction, life, and blessing—and never promotes sin, sickness, fear, or destruction. (**2 Tim. 3:16.**)

To dominate means to have or exert mastery, control, or preeminence.

Chapter 14
EXOUSIA POWER

"What is the exceeding greatness of his power to us-ward who believe, according to the working of his mighty power." **(Eph. 1:19.)**

When Jesus was raised from the dead, He gave us, the Church, *exousia* power. In other words, He *delegated empowerment* ("authorization") to use His name and His power!

Exousia is a Greek word (ἐξουσίαν) most often translated as "authority" or "power." It is especially used in terms of "influence." *Exousia* can also be thought of in terms of jurisdiction or dominion over a certain realm, right, privilege, or ability.

Exousia is used in the Gospel of Matthew and says, *"When Jesus had finished saying these things, the crowds were amazed at his teaching, because he taught as one who had authority [exousia], and not as their teachers of the law."* (**Matt. 7:28-29.**) The word is also used when Jesus demonstrates that He has "authority" to forgive sins by healing a paralyzed man (see **Matt. 9:6**).

In Ephesians, we see that Jesus is far above all authority, dominion, and power (see **Eph. 1:18–23**). In Colossians, it also affirms the supremacy of Jesus (see **Col. 1:15-20, Col. 2:10**). True *exousia* is His.

When Jesus commissioned His disciples, He gave them a measure of authority, too. In the Gospel of Mark, Jesus gives the Twelve authority, or *exousia*, over impure spirits when He sent the disciples out to preach (see **Mk. 6:7**).

The book of Ephesians talks about the, *"ruler of the kingdom [exousia] of the air, the spirit who is now at work in those who are disobedient."* (**Eph. 2:2**) However, this is not a ruler we need fear. Ephesians also says, *"[God's] intent was that now, through the church, the manifold wisdom of God should be made known to the rulers and authorities in the heavenly realms, according to his eternal purpose that he accomplished in Christ Jesus our Lord."* (**Eph. 3:10–11**.)

Ephesians further tells us that we struggle against those powers or authorities (see **Eph. 6:12**). Nonetheless, it also assures us that God has given us spiritual armor for the battle and that we can be strong in the Lord and His mighty power.

Colossians encourages, *"For he has rescued us from the dominion [exousia] of darkness and brought us into the kingdom of the Son he loves, in whom we have redemption, the forgiveness of sins."* (**Col. 1:13–14**.) Colossians also tells us that Christ has, *"disarmed the powers and authorities [exousia]"* and *"made a public spectacle of them, triumphing over them by the cross."* (**Col. 2:15**.) We battle a defeated foe because we serve the One who has authority over all (see **1 Cor. 15:20–28, 1 Pet. 3:21-b-22**).

We are in a Spiritual War

The finished work of Jesus, the Scriptures, Jesus' commission to the church, and the times in which we live all demand that we live in Jesus' power and in His authority. We cannot afford to neglect or marginalize this area of our lives. We are in a war, and we cannot ignore our enemy. Jesus never did.

The First Epistle of Peter says to be alert (see **1 Pet. 5:8**). Why? Because Satan, your adversary, roams around seeking to find people not just to give them a bad day, but also rather to devour and destroy them. If there was a predator in the physical world that wanted to destroy you, or if you were in a war zone and needed to go down the street to get some bread, you would be more alert than if you were in Disney World enjoying the rides.

Peter says, "Be alert," because Satan is out to destroy. We cannot be passive. We must exercise this power and authority to live free and triumphant. To have authority and not use it does not do us any good. We must appropriate it. I do not have to live mired underneath fear, self-hatred, and anger. Instead, I can live as the triumphant one.

Demonic spirits were a constant reality in Jesus' life, and that is no less the case today for us. We may not see them quite as obviously now. Our experience has been, though, especially over the last few years, that this is the case.

Whenever Jesus would show up somewhere, demonic spirits would make themselves known. Demonic spirits cannot rest underneath the presence of the light and the power of God. Darkness cannot overcome light; light always overcomes darkness.

> We are in a war, and we cannot ignore our enemy. Jesus never did.

If this room was filled with light, behind us was a room filled with darkness, and if we opened the doors, do you think the darkness would come in and put out the light in this room? Alternatively, would the light in this room go into the other room and dispel the darkness? When Jesus would show up, demons immediately could not handle the light and presence of God.

In the same way, as believers today move more into a ministry of power and authority, the demonic spirits are going to manifest. Moreover, when they reveal their hand, we have power and authority over them. We know how to set the captives free and to release the prisoners. It is a joy and very exciting to see people transformed. They are transformed because they have been near believers in the light—and they are set free!

Demonic spirits are just as real today, but the light of God is not as powerful in the westernized church as it ought to be. The westernized church makes peace with them, making them much more comfortable.

They just sit back, drink their soda, eat their chips, and let things go on. They are not "alert," "think" demons are not real or that they should be ignored,—and say, "let us just worship the Lord."

When the church of Jesus Christ recovers who it is, demonic spirits are not going to be comfortable. I want to make it as uncomfortable for them as possible by the truth that I believe and live. In the Church, there is much fear, because demonic spirits know that if they can get us filled with fear we are going to pull back and not be on our game.

I believe we are seeing demonic manifestations all around us.

* Would we call rampant divorce a demonic manifestation?

* Would we call large numbers of prodigal people running from God and from their physical parents a demonic manifestation?

* Would we call unbridled anger a demonic manifestation?

* Would we call abuse—physical, emotional, sexual, whatever it might be—a demonic manifestation?

* Would we call a perversion of how God created men and women, and rampant suicide—a demonic manifestation?

We may become fearful when we think of the demonic manifestations in the man in the region of the Gerasene (see **Mk. 5**). We do not want anything to do with that. Meanwhile the enemy is literally ravaging and shredding us because we do not want to acknowledge him and the need to fight him.

Jesus did not tolerate demonic manifestations. He exercised his authority in every way. We should do the same, because at salvation we enter Christ's authority.

Now let me give you a couple of practical ways that we might do this.

1. Should we always assume that a sickness, headache, sadness, or heaviness of spirit is not due to demonic activity? For Job, the source of his affliction was the enemy, and it could be the same with us. Because we do not consider the possibility that the enemy is at work, he has carte blanche, free access to keep exercising his devious deeds against us.

2. Do I have a humanistic, rationalistic way of thinking that will not allow me to consider such a possibility because I will look fanatical, like I have lost my mind, like I am just two steps away from an institution? We should at least stop and ask ourselves whether a problem could have a spiritual cause.

3. Demonic manifestations happen when a person prepares to do some type of ministry that is going to infringe upon the territory of the enemy. Demonic spirits are not going to lay back and say, "This is really interesting." No, they are going to oppose. Eighty years before Moses began to lead Israel out of Egypt, he was almost killed as an infant. Jesus lived thirty years before he began his earthly ministry and had an attempt on his life as an infant. The enemy is malicious and relentless enough to know his kingdom is going to be compromised by those who call themselves by the name of Jesus Christ. The enemy will oppose and resist one way or another.

4. Do not assume a string of misfortunes is not due to demonic activity against you. Enforce your authority.

5. Do not assume that relentless and powerful temptation is not due to demonic activity against you. Take up your dominion!

6. Do not think the enemy is not behind bad dreams that you or your family members suffer. Enforce your authority.

7. We labor under so much that is part of this spiritual realm, and we do not exercise the authority that Christ has given us.

Remember: the power that raised Jesus Christ from death is in you (see **Rom 8:11**). Subsequently, when you have prayed through the prayer of repentance, then you come to the stage of rebuking, resisting, and renouncing the enemy—do you think that a spiritual transaction happens? Oh yeah, you can take it to the bank, because the very power that raised Jesus from death is in you. When you speak, demons must obey—unless we give them a place to operate.

SPEAK TO YOUR MOUNTAIN

The most powerful gifts that God has given His children are often totally misunderstood. I believe that one of God's best gifts is the opportunity to speak to big problems, just as Jesus did!

In Mark Jesus instructed, *"whoever says to this mountain, 'Be removed and be cast into the sea,' and does **not doubt** in his heart, but believes that those things he says will be done, **he will have whatever he says.**"* (Mk. 11:23.)

* We release faith with words.

* We must believe what we say will come to pass.

* Train yourself to speak only what you are ready to believe.

* Speak 'to' problems, not about them.

* Say what you want, not what you have.

* When you speak negative things, you are activating trouble (see **Gal. 6:7**).

Exousia Power

* When you speak, you are planting seeds—good or bad.

* When you speak, you are signing a spiritual contract (see **Matt. 12:36-37**).

* With your spirit-led words, you can take dominion over sin, sickness, demons, and fear.

God has **empowered** believers with the "name of Jesus," the "Word of God," and the "Power of the Holy Spirit." Believers have been translated into God's **Kingdom**. We are empowered through the finished work of Jesus and given a restored position of authority and dominion (see **Col. 1:13**).

Jesus said the *Kingdom of God* is within you. If that is true, then we are *empowered* to bring good news, healing, and deliverance to the world (see **Lk. 17:20-21**).

Jesus gave us His Authority

Believers now have kingdom authority to rule and reign on Earth. The Gospel of Mark instructs us to demonstrate this "restored" authority (see **Mk 16, Matt. 16, and Rom. 5:17**).

> God has empowered believers with the "name of Jesus," the "Word of God," and the "Power of the Holy Spirit."

The plan of God has always been that God created the Earth, and He put Adam in charge. He created the Earth for His children to enjoy and dominate (see **Gen. 1:26, Ps. 115:16**).

The Earth still belongs to God, but Adam was the caretaker, having God's dominion over the Earth. Nevertheless, Adam sinned and gave his authority to Satan.

Jesus has restored and demonstrated the dominion and authority that Adam was supposed to walk in (see **Gen. 1:26-28**).

Jesus has given His authority to all born-again believers. Therefore, it is spiritually legal to imitate Jesus (see **Eph 5:1, Lk. 4:18**).

Here are Jesus' instructions to believers:

Luke says, so the Lord said, *"If you have faith as a mustard **seed**, you can say to this **mulberry tree**, 'Be pulled up by the roots and be planted in the sea,' and it would obey you."* (**Lk. 17:6**.)

Jesus also demonstrated how His disciples could lay hands on the sick, (see **Mk. 16:17-18**).

In Mark, they brought a blind man to Jesus, and begged Him to touch him (see **Mk. 8:22**). Consequently, He took the blind man by the hand and led him out of the town. Moreover, when He had spit on his eyes and put His hands on him, He asked him if he saw anything. And he looked up and said, "I see men like trees, walking." Then He put *His* hands on his eyes again and made him look up. Furthermore, he was restored and saw everyone clearly.

Matthew records Jesus' answer about cursing the fig tree:

> *"Jesus answered and said to them, "Assuredly, I say to you, if you have faith and do not doubt, you will not only do what was done to the fig tree, but also if you say to this mountain, 'Be removed and be cast into the sea,' it will be done."*
> **Matt. 21:21**

It is a Bible Principle

Speaking words from your heart is not new at all. God's spiritual laws have always been that way.

Romans explains how we are born-again: *"if you confess with your mouth the Lord Jesus and believe in your heart that God has raised Him from the dead, you will be saved."* (**Rom. 10:9**.)

If you do not fill your mind with God's Word—the enemy will fill it with fear, anxiety, stress, worry, and temptation.

Chapter 15
KEYS OF THE KINGDOM

"I will give you the keys of the kingdom of heaven, and whatever you bind on earth will be bound in heaven, and whatever you loose on earth will be loosed in heaven."
Matt. 16:19

Jesus was given all power in heaven and earth after He took the keys of dominion from Satan (see **Matt. 28:18**). After He was raised from the dead, Jesus delegated the keys of dominion to all believers.

The keys of the kingdom of heaven are to have authority and dominion on Earth!

The truth is that we are children and imitators of God (see **Eph. 5:1**). We are followers of Jesus. Therefore, when confronted with mountains of trouble, tribulation, sin, demons, or sickness—we should speak as Jesus would speak. He would command, declare, bind, and loose those that were held captive by the devil.

Remember, we are commanding the circumstances in Jesus' name, *"the gates of hades will not prevail against the church!"* (**Matt. 16:18**.)

It is the way Jesus would have us live. He took back the keys of the Kingdom from Satan—and gave them to us. The keys are "binding and loosing." Keys are used to lock and unlock doors and gates.

"I will give you the keys of the kingdom of heaven, and whatever you bind on earth will be bound in heaven, and

whatever you loose on earth will be loosed in heaven."
Matt. 16:19

In other words, we have been given **authority to bind** (not allow) demonic adversity, sin, sickness, and fear.

We have **authority and dominion to loose** (set free) people that are held captive by Satan. People can be loosed from addictions, grief, depression, sickness, and disease!

Now let us look at an example that Jesus demonstrated for us:

> *"Now He was teaching in one of the synagogues on the Sabbath. And behold, there was a woman who had a spirit of infirmity eighteen years, and was bent over and could in no way raise herself up. But when Jesus saw her, He called her to Him and said to her, "Woman, you are loosed from your infirmity." And He laid His hands on her, and immediately she was made straight, and glorified God."* **Lk. 13:10-13**

Let us look at another scripture that might be a surprise concerning the keys of the kingdom of heaven:

> *"He who sins is of the devil, for the devil has sinned from the beginning. For this purpose the Son of God was manifested, that He might **destroy** the works of the devil."* **1 Jn. 3:8**

This scripture gives one of the major purposes that Jesus came to Earth as an anointed man. In this scripture the word *destroy* is really translated from the Greek as "loose."

As we look back at the woman who was bent over for eighteen years, Jesus declared she was **loosed** from her infirmity. A wonderful demonstration of the keys of the Kingdom.

Now let us dive into another situation that Jesus used to demonstrate how to apply the "keys." Jesus was being accused of casting out demons by the power of Satan. Jesus answered,

> *"If I cast out demons by the Spirit of God, surely the kingdom of God has come upon you. Or how can one enter a **strong man's house** and plunder his goods, unless he first binds the strong man? And then he will plunder his house."* **Matt 12:28-29**

I now realize that the strongman is the devil. Although, what about "plundering his house?" Now I also realize, by the Spirit of God, that believers have the keys that will open the gates of hell—so that we can **bind** the strongman and **loose** the captives behind the gates.

Remember in the book Matthew? Jesus said, *"I will build My church, and the gates of Hades shall not prevail against it."* (**Matt. 16:18.**) The purpose of God is and was to establish His Kingdom on earth – first in men's hearts, then manifested in the physical realm.

Called to Conquer

The scriptures call believers *"more than conquerors."* (**Rom. 8:37.**) This statement is derived from the Greek word, *hupernikao*, which means, "to vanquish...gain a surpassing victory." In other words, God does not want us to survive merely; He wants us to experience a surpassing victory over the enemy of our souls. This victory is possible because Christ has already conquered the devil.

God does not want you to coexist with the powers of darkness—He wants you to conquer them! You are powerful! You are mighty! The greater One lives in you (see **1 Jn. 4:4, 1 Jn. 4:16-18**)!

Take It by Force!

We are called to conquer the enemy's kingdom and to seize our freedom by force. Whatever demonic oppression you refuse to drive out of your life will ultimately push you off the path of God's blessings.

Matthew instructs us, *"from the days of John the Baptist until now the kingdom of heaven suffers violence, and the violent take it by force."* **(Matt. 11:12.)**

God does not encourage us to use *physical* violence, but when it comes to *spiritual* warfare, we must employ force to overcome the devil and his works. The kingdom of darkness is energized by a show of fear and passiveness on the part of believers. We must realize what God has given us, and grab hold of God's promises by force—*"violent...force."*

The word *"violence"* in the cited Scripture previously mentioned comes from the Greek word *biazo*—to use force. The word *force* is defined as "strength or energy as an attribute of physical action or movement." Simply put, force is *power in action*.

Those who are willing to act will experience God's power, while those who remain passive will not experience freedom and victory.

What Will You Call It?

The first book to the Corinthians instructs us, *"Pursue love, and desire spiritual gifts, but especially that you may prophesy."* **(1 Cor. 14:1-2.)**

As we consider what the Lord has gifted us, we will discover that He also wants us to decree, prophesy, declare, profess, and speak to mountains of problems (see **Job 22:28** and **Matt. 21:21**).

We should also consider how the Lord God created us, *"Let Us make man in Our image, according to Our likeness..."* **(Gen. 1:26.)**

Plus, we are to be *"imitators of God as dear children."* **(Eph. 5:1.)**

As children of God, we can speak like God, *"who gives life to the dead and **calls those things** which do not exist as though they did,"* **(Rom 4:17b.)**

During a conversation or email, take an opportunity to **Prophesy:**

* I call you blessed.

* I call you anointed.

* I call your family restored.

* I call your family set-free.

* I call you prosperous.

* I call you a child of God.

* I call you healed.

* I call you faith filled.

* I call you Spirit-led.

* I call you an overcomer.

* I call you a conqueror!

The phrase, *"and calleth those things which be not as though they were,"* (**Rom. 4:17.**) is referring to the instance Paul had just cited when God changed Abram's name to Abraham (see **Gen. 17:5**). According to Strong's Concordance, the name Abram means "high father," and the name Abraham means "father of a multitude."

The Lord changed Abram's name to Abraham one year before the birth of Isaac, thus confessing that Abraham was the father of a multitude before it happened in the physical.

This illustrates God's faith. God says things are so before there is physical proof that they are so. The same thing was done at creation (see **Gen. 1:3**). God spoke everything into existence, and then it was so.

He spoke light into existence and then four days later created a source for that light to come from (see **Gen. 1:3, 14-19**).

God has given us the power to create with faith-filled words (see **Prov. 18:20-21, Mk. 11:14, 23**). If we are going to operate in God's kind of faith, we must learn to call those things that are not as though they were. (**Rom. 4:17b, KJV.**)

Abraham Considered Not

Romans tells us about faith:

> *"And not being weak in faith, he did not consider his own body, already dead (since he was about a hundred years old), and the deadness of Sarah's womb. He did not waver at the promise of God through unbelief, but was strengthened in faith, giving glory to God."* **Rom. 4:19-20**

The word "consider" is defined as "**1.** To think carefully about. **2.** To regard as. **3.** To take into account" (American Heritage Dictionary). The Greek word that was used here for "consider" is "katanoeo" and it simply means "to observe fully" (Strong's Concordance).

Therefore, we can see that Abraham did not think carefully about his age, and Sarah's, and the impact that it would have on the **promise** that God had given him. He did not consider those things or make any allowance for them. That was not what he paid attention to.

That is amazing, and that is exactly the reason many of us would not be able to receive the same **miracle.**

We consider every negative thing that looks **contrary** to God's promises, and then we try to use our faith to overcome the fear and unbelief that come with those thoughts, (see **Matt. 17:20**). That is not the way Abraham was strong in faith.

The first letter to the Corinthians tells us about things that are not:

*"God has chosen the foolish things of the world to put to shame the wise, and God has chosen the weak things of the world to put to shame the things which are mighty; and the base things of the world and the things which are despised God has chosen, and the **things which are not**, to bring to nothing the **things that are**."* **1 Cor. 1:27-28**

In the book of Acts, John and Peter 'called' a crippled man healed:

"In the name of Jesus Christ of Nazareth, rise up and walk." **(Acts. 3:6-b.)**

* I call my body healed.

* I call myself prosperous!

* I call myself disciplined.

* I call myself free from fear!

A left-handed pitcher hurled a fastball in the last inning, with two outs and two strikes.
The batter looked at the ump; the pitcher looked at the ump.
"What was it Mr. Umpire?"
The ump said, "It is nothing until I **call it**."

Put away every 'lame' excuse—believe God's promises, and get into a good 'Word' church.

Chapter 16
Breaking Demonic Strongholds

"The weapons of our warfare are not carnal but mighty in God for pulling down strongholds." (**2 Cor. 10:4.**)

Demonic strongholds are established for the sole purpose of keeping people oppressed, in bondage, and in captivity. This is the #1 strategy of the enemy of our soul. Every person alive has this same battle. The problem is that most people are living with oppression and doing nothing about it. (see **1 Jn. 5:19.**)

> Strongholds often manifest as thoughts, negative attitudes, imaginations, and doubting arguments.

Strongholds often manifest as thoughts, negative attitudes, imaginations, and doubting arguments. When the 'wicked one' tempts you, it is his plan to get you to buy his lies. The devil's strategy is to get you meditating on negative thoughts repeatedly until you start acting on those tempting thoughts.

Do not be fooled, the spiritual realm is real. On one hand, God, Jesus, Holy Spirit, angels, heaven, and everything that is good is trying to guide you into blessing and all the truth. On the other hand, there is Satan, demons, and everything that is bad for you is trying to *sway* you into addiction, sin, sickness, dementia, accidents, tragedy, disease, and unbelief (see **Jn. 10:10, 1 Jn. 5:19**, and **1 Pet, 5:8**).

How Strongholds Develop

Demonic strongholds are the only weapon that Satan has to defeat us. The truth is that *the tempter* gets people to agree with his lies. His lies are designed to go against and steal the Word of God that you hear (see **Mk. 4:15**).

The reason so many people are unable to break demonic strongholds is due to a lack of knowledge about how strongholds work. Satan builds a stronghold by starting with a simple thought. As he applies more and more tempting thoughts, people's defenses are weakened and finally, they begin acting on thoughts that will eventually manifest in addictive behavior with drugs, food, alcohol, sexual fantasies, and other life destroying habits.

In my life, a stronghold was trying to form through my younger years that I would die early as my father did. My father was only 34 years old when the devil came to steal, kill, and destroy (see **Jn. 10:10-a**). The devil's lies are always thoughts that are opposite of what the Word of God says. The Word tells us that by the stripes of Jesus we are *healed and forgiven*, which is the full gospel (see **1 Pet. 2:24**). My father only knew 'half' the gospel. He was not prepared to **war** against thoughts of disease, because he was not taught about God's gift of healing. Therefore, a stronghold of sickness was established, and he did not know how to fight back. Others of us must stand up against strongholds of family problems, addictions, and depression with truth that we know (see **Jn. 8:31-32**).

How to Break Strongholds

The term "stronghold" comes from the Greek word *ochuroma*, which means "castle" or "fortress". This is why we must *pull down* strong holds (see **2 Cor. 10:4**). The phrase "pulling down" comes from the Greek word *athairesis*, which means "destruction" or "demolition."

The only way to get rid of a stronghold in your life is to demolish it with the supernatural power of God's Word. You and I must be aggressive with God's Word, not passive. We must be willing to take the battering ram of the Word of God to break the walls of oppression set up by the powers of darkness.

Mighty Weapons

As believers, our weapons, are far more powerful than all the lies in the devil's arsenal.

The second letter to the Corinthians says it like this in the Amplified Bible:

> *"For the weapons of our warfare are not physical (weapons of flesh and blood), but they are mighty before God for the overthrow and destruction of strongholds."* **2 Cor. 10:4, AMP**

The word mighty comes from the Greek word *dunatos*, which means "able," "powerful" and "strong."

You may be dealing with strongholds of fear, weakness, shame, or condemnation. However, you have been given spiritual weapons that are powerful enough to break down and demolish any stronghold!

Casting Down Strongholds

Some of the problem with strongholds is that believers have become lazy. You are in a fight! The devil will try to strengthen his grip on you. He will try to add pressure to his grip on you; he is a liar and does not give up easily. Satan will use other people to reinforce his negative thoughts.

If you are struggling with a longtime sin or addiction, you may be dealing with a demonic stronghold. Call it out. Speak to it and cast it out in Jesus' name.

If there is a chronic sickness that seems to "run in the family," then you may be up against a demonic stronghold. Strongholds are persistent, long-lasting, life-controlling addictions, poverty, emotional turmoil, sexual perversion, anxiety, depression, sorrow, and fear. Call it out. Speak to it and cast it out in Jesus' name.

The second book of Corinthians tells us,

> *"casting down arguments and every high thing that exalts itself against the knowledge of God, bringing every thought into captivity to the obedience of Christ."* **2 Cor. 10:5**

The word *"arguments"* comes from the Greek word *logismos*, which means "reasoning." In other words, these arguments in the mind of a believer seem to be logical beliefs. Nevertheless, in fact, they can become strongholds against the truth of God's Word. Even religious traditions can be demonic strongholds (see **Mk. 7:13**).

Power of the Air

It is commonly taught that the devil and demonic host inhabit "hell." However, these wicked spiritual beings reside in the atmosphere, or the "second heaven."

The Epistle to the Ephesians says,

> *"In time past you walked according to the course of this world, according to the prince of the power of the air, the spirit that now wors in the children of disobedience."* **Eph. 2:2**

Satan is the prince of the power of the air. The word prince is from the Greek word *archon*, which means "ruler."

In other words, Satan is the *ruler of the air* in the spiritual realm. Satan's strategy is to manipulate the communication we receive from radio, television, music, computer, and all forms of media. Can you see why our media has been so wickedly corrupted?

The enemy's agenda is to rule and reign in the lives and minds of those who yield to his deception. No wonder the apostle Paul instructed us about the importance of *renewing our minds* to the will and Word of God (see **Rom 12:2**). The best way to live above the enemy's agenda is to regularly confess and declare the Word of God aloud.

Dominate In Life

The book of Romans helps us understand a bit further about dominion.

> *"For if by the one man's offense death reigned through the one, much more those who receive abundance of grace and of the gift of righteousness will reign in life through the One, Jesus Christ."* **Rom. 5:17**

This explains what happened when Adam bowed his knee to Satan's temptation in the Garden of Eden. *"Death reigned,"* means that death *dominated* mankind, in heart and soul. Although, after the finished work of Jesus born-again believers can *dominate in life* through Christ!

"The best way to live in victory is to confess, declare, and meditate God's Word." (Rom. 12:2.)

Chapter 17
Dominion from the 3rd Heaven

"He raised us up together and made us sit together in the heavenly places in Christ Jesus." (**Eph. 2:6**)

Would it not be awesome if we were far above all our problems? Unbelievably—it is possible when you are spiritually minded. Jesus sits at the right hand of God the Father; and spiritually, we believers have been raised up together to sit with Him. Today, Jesus is interceding for us; meaning, He is cheering for us to take our place as sons and daughters of God. Unfortunately, instead of viewing things from heaven's perspective, many Christians still focus on the natural things of this earth (see **Col. 3:1-4**).

Many Christians are so focused on the natural world that they forget Satan is the 'god' of this world and he wants to 'sway' us more and more into his domain (see **1 Jn. 5:19**). He is, *"the prince of the power of the air,"* (**Eph. 2:2.**) and a principality that we should be resisting with our dominion. Satan's number one weapon is deceit or deception. Believers should dominate what thoughts are let into their hearts!

Satan deceived Adam and Eve in the Garden. He succeeded in his strategy to get God's son and daughter to doubt what God had said. In Matthew he tried the same tactic against Jesus in the wilderness (see **Matt. 4:3**). Yet Jesus, the last Adam, refused to fall for the trap. Jesus was grounded in the truth of God's Word and would not doubt who He was as the Son of God.

Satan's tactic is always to get believers to doubt God's Word and to question the authority that we have in Christ. When Satan is successful, believers disqualify themselves in their own minds.

You Are Seated in Heavenly Places

As believers, we have not raised ourselves up by positive thinking, or higher education, or physical bodily exercise. Still, God himself has raised us up to sit together with Christ.

This is not thinking of ourselves above what we ought to. (**Rom. 12:3.**) Nevertheless, it is having a thankful, humble attitude—that receives what God has already done in the Spirit.

Some believers that have rejected what the Scriptures clearly say— and they think they are being humble by saying, "I'm just a worm," and "I'm just a sinner," and "I don't want to think that I am worthy." Of course, we are not worthy in ourselves, but God has **made** us worthy and made us spiritually alive in Christ (see **1 Cor. 15:22** and **Eph. 2:5**).

In fact, its 'false humility' for anyone to reject the high price Jesus paid for us to have power, authority, and dominion—in the earth and in the heavenly places.

Two Realms of Existence

A key to operating in third-heaven dominion understands the difference between the spiritual and physical realms. What we see, hear, and feel on this earth is all part of the physical realm.

The spiritual realm is made of what we cannot see—heaven, Jesus, the Holy Spirit, angels, demons, etc. (see **2 Cor. 3:18**). Of the two realms, the spiritual is always greater than the physical. Although we cannot see the spiritual realm with our natural eyes, the activity in the spirit manifests into what occurs in the physical.

God's kingdom in the spirit established His kingdom on the earth. *"God is a spirit, and those who worship Him must worship Him in spirit and truth."* (**Jn. 4:24**.) God, who is a spirit, created the physical universe. *"By faith we understand that the worlds were framed by the Word of God, so that the things which are seen were not made of things which were visible."* (**Heb. 11:3**.)

In other words, God created both the spiritual and physical realms, and it is the spiritual that gives life to the natural world.

When God created man, He uniquely designed him to exist in both realms simultaneously though His 3-part nature of spirit, soul, and body (see **1 Thess. 5:23**).

Your High Spiritual Position

From the position of being seated with Christ in heavenly places, you will be able to see everything around you from a brand-new perspective: you are not below the circumstances, but above them!

As you meditate on Ephesians, you will gain revelation knowledge of this third-heaven dominion—and it will radically change the way you pray, speak, declare, confess the Word, and dominate the circumstances (see **Eph. 2:6**). God has purposefully created you and me to conquer and dominate the works of darkness, in Jesus' mighty name!

Like an eagle, believers have been raised up together with Christ, and made to sit together in heavenly places in Christ Jesus.

Chapter 18
Dominion Releases God's Power

> *"And as you go, preach, saying, the kingdom of heaven is at hand. Heal the sick, cleanse the lepers, raise the dead, cast out devils: freely ye have received, freely give."* **Matt. 10:7-8**

There are several keys to seeing the miraculous power of God manifest on a consistent basis. One of the least understood, and therefore seldom practiced, is the fact that healing is under the authority of the believer. God has already provided His healing power and placed it on the inside of every born-again believer. It is up to us to release it. Understanding and using our authority is the key to seeing miracles happen.

Look at how Peter and John ministered healing to the lame man in Acts:

> *"Now Peter and John went up together into the temple at the hour of prayer, being the ninth hour. And a certain man lame from his mother's womb was carried, whom they laid daily at the gate of the temple which is called Beautiful, to ask alms of them that entered into the temple; Who seeing Peter and John about to go into the temple asked an alms. And Peter, fastening his eyes upon him with John, said, Look on us. And he gave heed unto them, expecting to receive*

something of them. Then Peter said, Silver and gold have I none; but such as I have give I thee: In the name of Jesus Christ of Nazareth rise up and walk. And he took him by the right hand, and lifted him up: and immediately his feet and ankle bones received strength. And he leaping up stood, and walked, and entered with them into the temple, walking, and leaping, and praising God." **Acts 3:1-8, KJV**

Notice that Peter did not pray for the man. He also did not ask God to heal him. He said, *"Such as I have give I thee."* **(Acts 3:6, KJV)** This did not mean that Peter was the source of this healing. Notice what Peter said in the Acts of the Apostles,

"And when Peter saw it, he answered unto the people, Ye men of Israel, why marvel ye at this? or why look ye so earnestly on us, as though by our own power or holiness we had made this man to walk?" **Acts 3:12, KJV**

God's power healed the man near the gate of the temple, but that power was under Peter's authority. Peter went on to say in verse 16 that it was faith in the name of Jesus that had wrought this miracle.

However, Peter did not ask God to heal this man. He believed the Lord had already done His part and had placed that power within him. Now it was Peter's responsibility to release that power, and that is just what he did.

The Lord never told us to pray for the sick in the sense that we ask Him to heal them. He told us to heal the sick. There is a big difference between the two. It has to do with operating in the authority He has already given us. Look at these commands the Lord gave His disciples.

"Then he called his twelve disciples together, and gave them power and authority over all devils, and to cure diseases.

Dominion Releases God's Power

> *And he sent them to preach the kingdom of God, and to heal the sick,"* **Lk. 9:1-2**

> *"And when he had called unto him his twelve disciples, he gave them power against unclean spirits, to cast them out, and to heal all manner of sickness and all manner of disease."* **Matt. 10:1**

> *"And as ye go, preach, saying, The kingdom of heaven is at hand. Heal the sick, cleanse the lepers, raise the dead, cast out devils: freely ye have received, freely give."* **Matt. 10:7-8**

Jesus told us to heal the sick, not pray for the sick. What a radical statement! This will get you kicked out of most churches today, but these are the exact words of our Lord Jesus Christ. In addition, this is precisely why more people do not see the miraculous results they are praying. They are not taking their authority and commanding God's power; they are passively asking God to do what He told them to do.

I know this goes contrary to popular Christian doctrine. We are constantly told that it is not us but God who is the Healer, and I agree with that totally. On the other hand, I also believe that God has placed His healing power under our authority, and it is up to us to release it. If we do not take our authority and become commanders instead of beggars, God's power will not be released. There needs to be a radical renewing of our thinking on this issue.

Look at an amazing passage of Scripture in the book of the prophet Isaiah.

> *"Thus saith the LORD, the Holy One of Israel, and his Maker, Ask me of things to come concerning my sons, and concerning the work of my hands command ye me."* **Isa. 45, 11, KJV**

What a powerful scripture! What does the Lord mean when He tells us to command Him? Well, He certainly does not mean we can order Him around. No! He means, concerning the "things" He has already done, He wants us to take His authority and command His power for helping people.

Using God's Power

It is like electricity. The power company generates the power and delivers it to your house. It is not your power, but it is under your control. You do not call the power company and ask them to turn the lights on. No!

They will not do that. They generate power, but it is under your command. You simply flip the switch on the wall and command the power to work. Does this mean you are the power source?—certainly not! You can put a light bulb in your mouth, and it will never come on.

You are not the power source, but you are the one in control of what that power does. You can plead with the power company all you want, but they will not flip the switch for you. You must assume your authority and acknowledge the power is under your command.

That is what the Lord was speaking. He has already healed everyone who will ever be healed. He did it two thousand years ago when He bore our stripes on His back. Then He deposited His resurrection power inside every believer (see **Eph. 1:19-20**). He has done His part, and now it is up to us to do ours.

We need to take the authority He has given us and become commanders instead of beggars. This powerful truth works. We are not just praying for the sick; we are healing them in Jesus' name.

This could revolutionize your whole approach toward the devil. Satan is not using some superhuman, angelic authority against us; he is using the authority and power that was given to man by God. Therefore, Satan cannot do anything to us without our consent and cooperation.

Established on the Word

You will dominate in life with faith that is established on the Word of God (see **1 Jn. 5:4**). Being established is a powerful scriptural principle. Becoming established does not happen overnight. You have to put in the time and effort to build your life on a solid spiritual foundation (see **Matt. 7:24-25**). Then make corrections to ensure you consistently resist temptation and build a good spiritual reputation with God against principalities and powers of wickedness. Living a transformed life will establish you in the spirit realm.

Your words become more powerful and effective when your words are established on God's Word. The spirit realm (and your own body) will become accustomed to responding to your words; positively or negatively (see **Prov. 18:21**).

In fact, your body will respond with healing as you speak to it as Jesus spoke healing to sick people. Jesus would say things like, "be healed," "take up your bed and walk," "receive your sight." On the other hand, if you always say things like, "I always get sick," "it is flu season and I will get it real soon," "my allergies will soon kick in." You are establishing a reputation in the spirit realm, and your body will respond according to what it consistently hears (see **Mk. 11:12-14, Mk .11:23**).

You have authority to take dominion because you are in Christ.

CHAPTER 19
DOMINION AND ANOINTING

"The Spirit of the Lord is upon me, because he hath anointed me." (**Lk. 4:18**)

Anointing, as described in the Bible, can be defined as "God on flesh doing those things that flesh cannot do." It is God doing those things only He can do, and doing them through a flesh-and-blood, earthly vessel, (see **2 Cor. 4:7**).

The basic meaning of the Bible word "anoint" is "to pour on, smear all over, or rub into." In the Old Testament, someone who was anointed by God for special service to God had oil poured or smeared on him.

For instance, the prophet Samuel anointed Saul, and later David, with oil when God revealed He had chosen him to be king of Israel. When King Saul rebelled against God and tried to kill David, David refused to harm him because Saul was *"the Lord's anointed."* (**1 Sam. 24:6.**)

To be anointed by God is not only to be picked, but also to be empowered by Him for the task or position to which He has called you.

The Hebrew word "Messiah" and the Greek word "Christ" both mean "the Anointed." In the New Covenant, Christ, the Anointed One, is listed more than 140 times. This Bible truth is enough to transform our entire Christian life – knowing that the word Christ is not

Jesus last name, or a title. Christ refers to the burden removing, yoke destroying power of God!

Anointing was always a sign of Israel's coming Redeemer. The prophet Isaiah, looking forward in time by the Spirit of God, saw One through Whom *"the yoke [of Satan's oppression] shall be destroyed because of the anointing."* (**Isa. 10:27**). The word destroyed means absolutely corrupted beyond use.

Jesus, reading from another Messianic prophecy in Isaiah, said,

> *"The Spirit of the Lord is upon me, because he hath anointed me..."* What had the Spirit anointed Him to do? *"To preach the gospel to the poor...heal the brokenhearted...preach deliverance to the captives and recovering of sight to the blind...set at liberty them that are bruised..."* **Lk. 4:18-19**

The Anointed One

Jesus had the burden-removing, yoke-destroying power of Almighty God all over Him. News of the Anointed and His Anointing was the "good news" or "gospel" the early Church ministered.

When Peter was asked to preach the basic, gospel message to the Gentiles for the very first time, the first thing he told them was,

> *"how God anointed Jesus of Nazareth with the Holy Ghost and with power: who went about doing good, and healing all that were oppressed of the devil; for God was with him."* **Acts 10:38-39**

When Philip preached Christ (the Anointed One and His Anointing) in Samaria,

> *"the people with one accord gave heed unto those things which Philip spoke, hearing and seeing the miracles which*

he did. For unclean spirits, crying with loud voice, came out of many that were possessed with them: and many taken with palsies, and that were lame, were healed." **Acts 8:6-8**

They received and heard the good news that the Anointed One and His Anointing had come to destroy the yokes from their backs. From the moment they received it, God confirmed it, just as He did in Jesus' ministry.

The anointing goes side by side with God's presence in the Holy Spirit. The anointing on Jesus was with the Holy Spirit (see **Lk. 4:18; Acts 10:38**).

The anointing we have received from Jesus is side by side with the Holy Spirit (see **1 Jn. 2:20, 26-27; Jn. 14:26**). The anointing is God's Spirit and power for service in this earth.

The Anointed One

The word "Christ" is not just another name for Jesus, but also a reference to the Anointed One and the Anointing that was on Him and in Him.

In the same way, the word "Christians" means more than just followers of Jesus. It means "the anointed."

The same yoke-destroying Anointing that was on Jesus is available to you. Look again at the First Epistle of John:

> *"the anointing which ye have received of him abideth in you, and ye need not that any man teach you: but as the same anointing teacheth you of all things, and is truth, and is no lie, and even as it hath taught you, ye shall abide in him."*
> **1 Jn. 2:27, KJV**

Those last two words could also be translated "in it." In other words, the phrase could either be exhorting believers to abide in the Anointed

One, Jesus, or to abide in the anointing itself. Both interpretations are correct because you cannot separate the Anointed and the anointing. If you are in the Anointed One, then you are in the anointing.

I encourage you; find every reference that uses the word Christ in the New Testament. Each time Christ is used translate it into "the Anointed and His Anointing." Then meditate on the new revelation of this meaning in each scripture. Start with the verses that say, "in Christ" or "through Christ" and translate them, "in (through) the Anointed and (through) His Anointing." It will change your life!

You Are Anointed

If you are "in Christ," there is an anointing for everything you are called to do, no matter how small or how great the task. That is what the Apostle Paul meant when he said, *"I can do all things through Christ (the Anointed and His Anointing) which strengthened me."* (**Phil. 4:13.**) Notice that he did not say, "who strengthened me" but "which strengthened me." He was talking about the anointing. The same anointing that enabled you to be born again will heal your body, help you succeed in business, and empower you to prosper in spirit, soul, body and in every aspect of your life (see **Lk. 5:20-24**).

Obedience is the key for functioning in the anointing. The final factor led through the final downfall of King Saul. In the first book of Samuel, Saul became impatient and took it upon himself to make a sacrifice rather than wait for Samuel to arrive (see **1 Sam. 13:8-15**). Some of Saul's men had already begun to defect. When Samuel arrived, Saul said, in his own defense, that he "felt *compelled*" to do what he did (see **1 Sam. 13:12,** emphasis added).

That is the negative side of an, "unction to function"—doing what seems right to you without the anointing. Samuel rebuked Saul, telling him that he had acted foolishly, and had not kept the commandment of the Lord.

The main rule for having authority is also to be under authority yourself, and that starts with being obedient to the Lord.

Even Jesus remarked that He had not found such great faith in Israel when he encountered the centurion in the book of Matthew (see **Matt. 8**). When Jesus told him that He would come and heal his servant, the centurion humbly said,

> *"Lord, I am not worthy that You should come under my roof. But only speak a word, and my servant will be healed."*

He continued,

> *"For I also am a man under authority, having soldiers under me. And I say to this one, 'Go,' and he goes; and to another, 'Come,' and he comes; and to my servant, 'Do this,' and he does it."* **Matt 8-9**

Now that is a true picture of *meekness*, a gentle humility that demonstrates power under control.

Going back to Saul, the final blow came when he disobeyed the word of the Lord spoken through Samuel to destroy the Amalekites (see **1 Sam. 15:1-3**). Saul was instructed to attack King Agag and the Amalekites and not spare anything alive: *"Kill both man and woman, infant and nursing child, ox and sheep, camel and donkey"* (**1 Sam. 15:3**). Except, Saul spared the best the Amalekites had, including the king himself. He then told Samuel "the people" had saved the animals to sacrifice (see **Sam. 15: 9, 13-15**). In rebuke, Samuel said,

> *"Has the Lord as great delight in burnt offerings and sacrifices, as in obeying the voice of the Lord? Behold, to obey is better than sacrifice, and to heed than the fat of rams. For rebellion is as the sin of witchcraft.* **1 Sam. 15:22-23**

That very day the Lord tore the kingdom of Israel away from Saul (see **1 Sam. 15:28**).

Obedience is a Key

The unction to function in the anointing of God works within the framework of obedience. God is more interested in our character than our comfort. He is raising up a generation that will *do what He says* in the *correct way*, which will achieve His objective and bring glory to Him—not build up our own egos.

In these last days, we must be people and ministers of integrity, honesty, and humility. We must go beyond just knowing the principles of the kingdom; we must also know the King—His will, His ways, His very heartbeat. And again, this is possible because we have "an *unction* from the Holy One, as ye know all things" (**1 Jn. 2:20, KJV**, emphasis added). The Lord Himself enables us to possess knowledge of the *truth*, because He is the living Word.

Daniel declares, "*The people who know their God shall be strong, and carry out great exploits.*" (**Dan. 11:32**.) It is time to function in the anointing with the right spirit and with power from on high: "God's X Factor," the unction to function that moves us to obey Him and release a mighty anointing in the earth.

The same God who does the work in all of us anoints you to flow in special abilities that have been tailor-made for you. You can obey God and move in the anointing, whether you are laboring alone or working together with your brothers and sisters in Christ. You can hear, obey, and flow in the anointing of God—fearlessly, favorably, and fiercely.

Believers have dominion over Satan and circumstances.

CHAPTER 20
WHAT DOMINION REALLY MEANS

"Then God blessed them, and God said to them, Be fruitful and multiply; fill the earth and subdue it; have dominion." **(Gen. 1:28)**

We have dominion on the Earth! Given by God to mankind from the beginning (see **Gen. 1:26-28**), our dominion is not to rule over other people; Instead, we are meant to have authority over every situation—physical, financial, emotional, and spiritual. In other words, believers have dominion over sin, sickness, demons, and fear!

Most Christians do not boldly take their place in a position of dominion because it is little preached or—studied. In fact, many Ministers preach against having dominion—why?

When you develop a deeper understanding of dominion, you will build the confidence you need to operate in it every day, in every area of your life.

Then God said,

> *"Let us make human beings in our image, to be like us. They will reign over the fish in the sea, the birds in the sky, the livestock, all the wild animals on the earth, and the small animals that scurry along the ground."* **Gen 1:26, NLT**

> *Then God blessed them, and God said to them, "Be fruitful and multiply; fill the earth and subdue it; have dominion over the fish of the sea, over the birds of the air, and over every living thing that moves on the earth,"* **Gen. 1:28**

1. Dominion Means Operating in the Anointing

According to **Psalm 8:6** we know of the Lord God: "You have made him to have dominion over the works of Your hands; You have put all things under his feet."

Jesus Himself (the anointed One) gave us the truth of the gospel (the Good News) when He quoted:

> *"The Spirit of the LORD is upon Me, Because He has anointed Me To preach the gospel to the poor; He has sent Me to heal the brokenhearted, To proclaim liberty to the captives And recovery of sight to the blind, To set at liberty those who are oppressed."* **Lk. 4:18**

Because Christ is in you—the same anointing that Jesus had in the book of Luke will bring healing, freedom, and anointing to many who you pass by in your daily routine. As the scripture says,

> *"God anointed Jesus of Nazareth with the Holy Spirit and with power, who went about doing good and healing all who were oppressed by the devil, for God was with Him."* **Acts 10:38**

And as we submit ourselves to the Lord our God we can confidently pray, *"Direct my steps by Your word, and let no iniquity have dominion over me."* **(Ps. 119:13,)**

2. Dominion Means Excelling to the Highest Place Possible

"Behold, I have given you authority to tread on serpents and scorpions, and over all the power of the enemy, and nothing shall hurt you." (**Lk. 10:19, ESV**)

"The heaven, even the heavens, are the LORD's; But the earth He has given to the children of men." (**Ps. 115:16.**)

"For sin shall not have dominion over you, for you are not under law but under grace." (**Rom. 6:14.**)

* Let the dominion and authority that belongs to you in Christ Jesus become a revelation on the inside of you. Believe it and use it in every situation. You never have to be a victim again.

* Dominion and authority are not a feeling—they are by faith.

* Dominate the circumstances, emotions, physical body, mental stability, and the Earth.

* We are dealing with things that have not been on the Earth ever before—destroying every yoke.

3. Dominion Means Expecting to Be Healed

   "They overcame him by the blood of the Lamb and by the word of their testimony, and they did not love their lives to the death." (**Rev. 12:11.**)

   "He sent His word and healed them And delivered them from their destructions." (**Ps. 107:20.**)

"Knowing that Christ, having been raised from the dead, dies no more. Death no longer has dominion over Him." **(Rom. 6:9.)**

4. Dominion Means Destroying Every Yoke

"For assuredly, I say to you, whoever says to this mountain, 'Be removed and be cast into the sea,' and does not doubt in his heart, but believes that those things he says will be done, he will have whatever he says." **Mk. 11:23**

"For if by the one man's offense death reigned through the one, much more those who receive abundance of grace and of the gift of righteousness will reign in life through the One, Jesus Christ." **Rom. 5:17**

"For You have broken the yoke of his burden And the staff of his shoulder, The rod of his oppressor, As in the day of Midian." **(Isa. 9:4.)**

"It shall come to pass in that day That his burden will be taken away from your shoulder, And his yoke from your neck, And the yoke will be destroyed because of the anointing oil." **Isa. 10:27**

"Come to Me, all you who labor and are heavy laden, and I will give you rest. Take My yoke upon you and learn from Me, for I am gentle and lowly in heart, and you will find rest for your souls. For My yoke is easy and My burden is light." **Matt. 11:28-30**

"Now, Lord, look on their threats, and grant to Your servants that with all boldness they may speak Your word," **(Acts 4:29.)**

"And when they had prayed, the place where they were assembled together was shaken; and they were all filled with the Holy Spirit, and they spoke the word of God with boldness." **Acts 4:31**

"Let us therefore come boldly to the throne of grace, that we may obtain mercy and find grace to help in time of need." **(Heb. 4:16.)**

"The wicked flee when no one pursues, But the righteous are bold as a lion." **(Prov. 28:1.)**

Walking Deeper in the Spirit

All the holy scriptures are God-breathed and declare God's plan for humanity. God created man in His image and likeness and gave him dominion. Adam lost this image, likeness, and dominion. Even though, God had a plan to get it back.

Jesus' death was far more than just the ending of sin—it was also the beginning of new creation: sons and daughters! Now, as new creations in Christ, we all can partake in the new covenant that the Father has established with Jesus. *"For whom He foreknew, He also predestined to be conformed to the image of His Son, that He might be the firstborn among many brethren."* **(Rom. 8:29.)**

Jesus did not come to be the only one; He came to be the first one among many others. God the Father was after His original plan for humanity that He purposed in Adam—sons and daughters in His image and likeness.

Jesus came to earth to reveal to humankind our identity, authority, and glory and restore it back to us. Jesus came to demonstrate dominion and break the power of sin and Satan over our lives. We were never created to have sin and wickedness in us. We were supposed to be God's offspring. When you see Jesus in the Earth realm, you are looking at the true potential of God's plan for man.

No wonder Jesus did so many miracles, healings, and deliverances. He was demonstrating the dominion that mankind should have had all along! Jesus demonstrated (see **Gen. 1:27-28**).

Jesus also demonstrated the dominion plan of God in the Gospel of Mark (see **Mk. 11:20-22**). He cursed the fig tree, as He continued to teach about dominion, He said:

> *"For assuredly, I say to you, whoever says to this mountain, 'Be removed and be cast into the sea,' and does not doubt in his heart, but believes that those things he says will be done, he will have whatever he says."* **Mk. 11:23**

The first part of a particular verse from the book of Matthew records what Jesus said, *"I will give you the keys of the kingdom of heaven."* (**Matt. 16:19-a**).

Now, are you ready to walk deeper in the Spirit? Go ahead say, "Yes and Amen!"

You will experience as much of God's power as you can believe, speak, and receive.

Chapter 21
THE TRUTH ABOUT DOMINION

"Behold, I give you the authority." (**Lk. 10:19**)

As new creations, we have been put in a position of dominion and authority—a position delegated to us by God through Jesus Christ. Along with that authority come certain responsibilities. I want us to examine God's Word concerning that position and the dominion we have in Him. *(For all intents and purposes, dominion is the same as authority in Christ.)*

When you made Jesus Christ the Lord of your life, the Epistle to the Colossians says you were delivered from the power of darkness (see **Col. 1:13**). The word power is literally translated authority. As well as, authority also means dominion.

You have been delivered from the power, or authority, of darkness and placed into God's kingdom. Jesus said, *"All power is given unto me in heaven and in earth. Go ye therefore..."* (**Matt. 28:18-19**.) That power was given to you as part of your inheritance in Christ Jesus. You have entered this position of authority because you are "in Christ."

The Word says that righteousness has come upon all men (see **Rom. 5:18**). You may ask, "Then why don't all become righteous?" To 'receive' it, you have to 'act' on righteousness from the point of authority.

In 1975, I used my dominion and authority as a human being and made a choice. I made the decision to receive Jesus as Lord of my life.

At that moment, I was made righteous in Christ. (I did not earn it or deserve it, Jesus did it for me.)

The book of second Corinthians says, *"He hath made him to be sin for us, who knew no sin; that we might be made the righteousness of God in him."* (**2 Cor 5:21.**)

5 Truths About Dominion and Authority

#1 – Jesus Secured Our Power, Authority, and Dominion

Jesus succeeded in securing all power by going to the cross, dying a horrible death, suffering the penalty for sin, and defeating Satan in the pit of hell. He came to earth as a man for one reason: to re-capture the authority that Satan had stolen through Adam's disobedience in the garden. Jesus was called the last Adam (see **1 Cor. 15:45**). After securing that power and authority, He freely gave it over into the hands of those who would believe in Him—that is, you and me.

It is not enough for us to accept Jesus' work at Calvary. We are held responsible for much more. Jesus' words in the Gospel of Mark were not intended for the early church alone (see **Mk. 16:17-18**). His words are just as vital and real today as when they were first spoken.

Jesus appeared to His disciples after His resurrection from the dead. His words to them form the foundation for the work of the New Testament church. It was at that time that He delegated the authority to carry out that work. Beginning in **verse 15**, Jesus said:

> *"Go ye into all the world and preach the gospel to every creature. He that believeth and is baptized shall be saved; but he that believeth not shall be damned. And these signs shall follow them that believe; In my name shall they cast out devils; they shall speak with new tongues; They shall take up serpents; and if they drink any deadly thing, it shall not*

hurt them; they shall lay hands on the sick, and they shall recover." **Mk. 16:15**

Go ye into the entire world and preach the gospel to every creature. Every born-again believer has the authority and responsibility to preach the Gospel of Jesus Christ in this earth. If you cannot go, then you can send someone in your place.

As well as, these signs shall follow them that believe…I want you to know who is to do all these things.

The signs will follow the believers who act in faith and boldly speak in Jesus' name. They shall cast out devils; they shall speak with new tongues; they shall lay hands on the sick, etc. The believer is the one with the power and authority to do these things.

The book of Mark says, *"They went forth, and preached everywhere, the Lord working with them, and confirming the word with signs following."* (**Mk. 16:20.**) God will confirm His Word, but first it must be put forth. That is where you and I come in. God does not preach; He has given us the authority to do the preaching. God will not lay hands on the sick. He will bring the healing, but you and I as believers must lay hands on the sick by faith, believing that God will perform His Word.

#2 – We Have Dominion to Stand Against Satan

One of the most vital areas of the believer's authority is God's power to stand successfully against Satan.

The book of Ephesians says, *"Neither give place to the devil."* (**Eph. 4:27.**) In the sixth chapter of Ephesians, the Apostle Paul describes the armor that we as believers are to wear in combat against Satan. He explains each piece of that armor. It is the armor of God. Except, not once does he say that God will put the armor on you or that God will fight the devil for you.

'You' is the understood subject of these verses. Paul says things like this,

> *"You be strong in the Lord. You put on the whole armor of God that you will be able to stand against the wiles of the devil. You take the whole armor of God that you may be able to withstand in the evil day; and having done all, you stand."* **Eph 6:10-18**

God has given you the power and the authority to stand against Satan and his destructive works. He has provided the armor, but it is your responsibility as a believer to put on that armor and stand against the devil. James says, you resist the devil, and he will flee from you (see **Jas. 4:7**). The armor and the weapons are at your disposal. God is there with you to back His Word; but all is worthless unless you take your position of authority and assume the responsibility to use what He has provided.

You have the power and the authority to take the Word of God, the name of Jesus, and the power of the Holy Spirit, and run Satan out of your affairs. Do not pray and ask God to fight Satan for you. You are the one in authority. Take your responsibility, speak directly to Satan yourself, and stand your ground firmly. He will flee!

God's power is in His Word. He is upholding all things by the word of His power (see **Heb. 1:3**). You need to learn to minister and walk from a point of authority. In His earthly ministry, Jesus said such things as "Be thou made whole." "Take up your bed and walk." Then to a lame man, Peter said in Acts, *"In the name of Jesus Christ of Nazareth rise up and walk."* (**Acts. 3:6.**) He too ministered and spoke from a point of authority.

Jesus came to earth as a man for one reason: to re-capture the authority that Satan had stolen through Adam's disobedience in the garden.

Now is the Time

It is time for you as a believer to begin to act that way. You have obtained an inheritance, and in that inheritance, you have been given all authority. The God of the universe lives inside you! He lives and walks in you. Become God inside minded and you will begin to walk in this point of authority.

Keep right on building yourself up in your inheritance. You live in a world that is full of evil influences. Satan wants to see to it that you forget the reality of being born again. He wants to see to it that you never realize your place of authority in Christ Jesus, because if you do, that power you walk in makes you dangerous to him. He has no defense against you when you walk in the power of God's Word.

When you see in the Word that you are in Christ Jesus, which you are in Him, confess it with all your heart. Then you will be strong, standing in a point of authority and operating in your inheritance in Him. As you do this, the power of God will always be available to work in your behalf. Praise God!

#3 – We Are Seated with Him in Dominion

In Ephesians, Paul prayed a prayer for the body of believers in Ephesus. One part of that prayer was that they know the exceeding greatness of his power to those who believe (see **Eph. 1:19**). That exceedingly great power is the same power that God used to raise Jesus from the dead and set Him at His own right hand in heaven. Ephesians tells us that Jesus is seated far above all principality, and power, and might, and dominion, and every name that is named (see **Eph. 1:21**).

The work God did in Jesus was supreme. He raised Jesus from the dead and set Him far above all other authority—not only in this world, but also in the heavenly world. Then in the following verse from the passage previously mentioned, says that God has put ALL things under His feet and made Him head over the church which is His body. Where are the feet? They are in the body. As believers, we are part of His body, and we are seated with Him in that highly exalted place of authority. Praise God! Look at Ephesians, chapter two:

> *"And you hath he quickened, who were dead in trespasses and sins...Even when we were dead in sins, (God) hath quickened us together with Christ...And hath raised us up together, and made us sit together in heavenly places in Christ Jesus."* **Eph. 2:1, 5, 6**

We are seated together with Him—where? Far above all principality, power, might, and dominion; as a believer, you have accepted the substitutionary sacrifice of Jesus at Calvary.

Therefore, you are a part of His body and are seated with Him in that heavenly place, equipped with the same power, the same authority that He has.

The great power that God worked in Christ when He raised Him from the dead is the same creative power of God that worked in you to make you alive when you were dead in your trespasses and sins.

The moment you made Jesus Christ the Lord of your life, that same power was exercised on your dead, unregenerate spirit, causing it to be reborn in the likeness of God Himself. Any man who is in Christ Jesus is a new creation: old things have passed away, all things are new, and all things are of God (see **2 Cor. 5:17**).

As believers, we are part of His body, and we are seated with Him in that highly exalted place of authority.

#4 – We Have the Power

> *"On the same day, when evening had come, He said to them, "Let us cross over to the other side." Now when they had left the multitude, they took Him along in the boat as He was. And other little boats were also with Him. And a great*

> *windstorm arose, and the waves beat into the boat, so that it was already filling. But He was in the stern, asleep on a pillow. And they awoke Him and said to Him, "Teacher, do You not care that we are perishing?" Then He arose and rebuked the wind, and said to the sea, "Peace, be still!" And the wind ceased and there was a great calm. But He said to them, "Why are you so fearful? How is it that you have no faith?"* **Mark 4:35-40**

Jesus spoke the words, let us pass over unto the other side, and there was enough power and authority in those words to accomplish the job. One thing I want you to notice is that Jesus did not take command of the ship to see that His words were carried out. He walked to the back of the boat and went to sleep.

Jesus delegated the authority to His disciples, and they accepted it. Except, when the storm came, they were filled with fear that the boat would sink and Jesus had to carry out the responsibility of authority that he had delegated to them by rebuking the wind and the sea.

You have the power and the authority to take the Word of God, the name of Jesus, and the power of the Holy Spirit and run Satan out of your affairs.

I want you to see the parallel here. You are the captain of your ship. You have control over your own life–your spirit, your soul, and your body. Jesus has delegated power or authority over Satan to you as a believer. You are to give him no place in your life. You are born of the Spirit of God. You are filled with the Spirit of God. You have been given the Word of God. Those three elements are enough for you to carry out your spiritual authority here in the earth.

You do not need any more power. You have all the power necessary. You simply must enforce your authority. Jesus has already done everything necessary to secure the authority and power over sin, sickness, demons, and fear. You must energize the faith action to receive that authority and join forces with Him in this earth. You are the one to be strong in the Lord and in the power of His might.

#5 – We Have Authority to Act as New Creations

Hebrews says,

> *"For as much then as the children are partakers of flesh and blood, he also himself likewise took part of the same. Jesus partook of flesh and blood, so that you could partake of spirit and life. For you to partake of that spirit and life, you must take the responsibility of standing in the place of authority as the new creation in Christ Jesus that you are."* **Heb. 2:14**

You are born again, not of corruptible seed, but of incorruptible, by the Word of God (see **1 Pet. 1:23**). The Word of Almighty God was injected into your spirit to bring about the new birth in your life. When the church was first beginning, the book of Acts described it as the Word growing and multiplying (see **Acts 12:24**). The Word is in you, but you are the one who must be willing to allow it to work in you.

Ephesians says,

> *"if indeed you have heard Him and have been taught by Him, as the truth is in Jesus: that you put off, concerning your former conduct, the old man which grows corrupt according to the deceitful lusts, and be renewed in the spirit of your mind, and that you put on the new man which was created according to God, in true righteousness and holiness."* **Eph. 4:21-24**

You are the one in authority. It is your responsibility to put off the old man–the unregenerate man that you were before you accepted Jesus. The Holy Spirit does the actual work in you, but you must make the decision to allow Him to do it. God has never forced His will on any person. You put off the old man. 'You' use the Word of God to renew your mind. You put on the new man, which is created in righteousness and true holiness.

In Jesus' Name, I Have Dominion over Sin, Sickness, Demons, and Fear; (when I am In Christ).

Chapter 22
3 KEYS TO KINGDOM LIVING

"He who is in you is greater than he who is in the world." (**1 Jn. 4:4**)

3 Keys to Empowered Living:

1. Enforcing Dominion IN JESUS' NAME

Nothing in this world is more powerful than the name of Jesus—why? ...because it is the key, or the "password," to our dominion as believers. The Bible says we have already been given *"every spiritual blessing in the heavenly places in Christ."* (**Eph. 1:3.**)

Think of it: every spiritual blessing already belongs to us. The question is, how do we access these blessings and apply them to our lives?—through faith in the name of Jesus!

In Jesus' name, we have dominion over any virus, cancer, or other disease that attacks our body. We can say, "Stop, in the name of Jesus! You will go no further." The enemy must obey when we stand in the authority and power of Jesus' name. Paul tells us, *"that at the name of Jesus every knee will bow...every tongue will confess that Jesus Christ is Lord, to the glory of God the Father."* (**Phil. 2:10-11, NASB**)

Every demon will have to bow before His name. Every problem will have to bow to the name of Jesus. Every financial need will have to bow. Every divisive spirit will have to bow!

The power, dominion, and authority delegated to you in Jesus' name does not make you immune to the enemy's attacks. However, it does give you the ability to overcome them. John wrote, *"He who is in you is greater than he who is in the world."* (**1 Jn. 4:4.**) You can live in victory in the name of Jesus!

No wonder the devil hates to hear that name. No wonder he does everything he can to discredit it, ridicule it, and water it down. As a result, some believers have lost their boldness to use the name of Jesus. They do not mind speaking to their unsaved friends about "God" or their "higher power," but they are intimidated from declaring their confidence in the name of Jesus.

Despite lacking our modern conveniences, the early church turned the world upside down for Jesus. (see **Acts 17:5-7**). In just a few centuries, they had spread the gospel to the known world. From Jesus' original handful of followers, the community of faith had grown to millions.

What was the secret of the early Christians? I am sure several things could be cited as reasons for their success; but one stands out above them all: They understood the power they had in the name of Jesus! Look at these amazing examples: On the day of Pentecost, Peter preached, *"Whoever calls on the name of the Lord shall be saved."* (**Acts 2:21.**)

In its simplest terms, the gospel is summed up by offering individuals who call on the name of Jesus to be saved. Peter told the new converts to repent and, *"be baptized in the name of Jesus Christ for the remission of sins."* (**Acts 2:38.**) From the first moment of their salvation, these believers were transferred into God's kingdom by Jesus' name.

The lame man sitting outside the temple was told, *"In the name of Jesus Christ of Nazareth, rise up and walk."* (**Acts 3:6.**) He was healed through the power of faith in Jesus' name.

Reclaiming the Power of His Name Despite the overwhelming evidence of how the early church unleashed God's miracle-working power through the name of Jesus, we have somehow drifted far from this practice today. Yes, we put "in the name of Jesus" at the end of our prayers, but do we truly believe in the power of that name?

Look at what the Bible says about the name of Jesus:

Jesus' name was prophesied and confirmed by God Himself. Two verses in Isaiah specifically mention the "name" of the coming Messiah: *"Therefore the Lord Himself will give you a sign: behold, the virgin shall conceive and bear a Son, and shall call His name Immanuel."* (**Isa. 7:14.**) Matthew quotes this Old Testament prophecy in relationship to Jesus, and he mentions that the meaning of Immanuel is *"God with us."* (**Matt. 1:23.**)

2. Enforcing Dominion in GOD'S WORD

Just as we have dominion in the name of Jesus, we also have dominion when we stand on God's Word. Satan does not tremble when we share our opinions and theories. Nor does he flee just because we can quote some sermon by our pastor or a TV preacher. In fact, the devil does get scared when he sees that we are grounded in the truth of Scripture and able to demolish his lies.

The truth will set us free from Satan's snares (see **Jn. 8:32**), and the truth is found in God's Word.

Do you or a loved one need healing or deliverance today? The Bible says, *"[God] sent His word and healed them and delivered them from their destructions."* (**Ps. 107:20.**) We are told to give attention to God's words, because *"they are life to those who find them, and health to all their flesh."* (**Prov. 4:22.**)

Jesus has a prescription for you, and it is found in His Word. Are you facing troubling circumstances in your life? One word from Jesus can calm your raging storm (see **Mark 4:35-41**). The disciples were so terrified about their circumstances that they said to Jesus, *"Teacher,* *do You not care that we are perishing?"* (**Mk. 4:38.**) Still, after the Lord spoke peace to their circumstances, *"the wind ceased and there was a great calm."* (**Mk. 4:39.**) At this point, Jesus scolded His disciples for not exercising their own faith to calm the storm: *"Why are you so fearful? How is it that you have no faith?"* (**Mk. 4:40.**)

God has given you His Word to speak to your troublesome situations today. Whether you need a healing, a financial breakthrough, the salvation of a loved one, or some other prayer answered, remember this: You have been given dominion and authority to speak God's Word to the "mountain" you face!

When God speaks, miracles happen, as David describes so graphically in Psalms:

> *"The God of glory thunders; the Lord is over many waters. The voice of the Lord is powerful; the voice of the Lord is full of majesty. The voice of the Lord breaks the cedars, yes, the Lord splinters the cedars of Lebanon. He makes them also skip like a calf, Lebanon and Sirion like a young wild ox. The voice of the Lord divides the flames of fire. The voice of the Lord shakes the wilderness; the Lord shakes the Wilderness of Kadesh. The voice of the Lord makes the deer give birth, and strips the forests bare; and in His temple everyone says, Glory!"* **Ps. 29:3-9**

Your circumstances will be transformed when you read God's Word, hear His voice, and then speak His promises!

The Word Brings Victory

In the context of describing the wonderful armor God has given us to ward off the devil's attacks (see **Eph. 6: 10-17**), Paul described God's Word as *"the sword of the Spirit."* (**Eph. 6:17.**) While the helmet, shield, and other pieces of armor are basically defensive in nature, the sword is the only offensive weapon described in this passage. We see Jesus using the Word as a sword in His encounter with Satan in the wilderness at the start of His ministry. He used this sword to counteract each of the devil's three attacks: *"It is written..." was His reply each time."* (**Lk. 4:1-13.**)

Notice that Jesus did not have to do a lot of scriptural research to discern and defeat Satan's lies. He already knew the Word and was ready to go to battle!

Can the same be said about you? Do you know God's Word well enough to counteract the enemy's lies? Can the Holy Spirit work through you to wield this mighty weapon as a "sword" to destroy Satan's strongholds?

I encourage you to commit yourself to taking time each day to study and meditate on God's promises in the Bible. There is no other way to stand in God's authority and be successful in spiritual warfare.

Exposing Satan's Lies

To understand how the Word of God enables us to defeat Satan's attacks, we need to recognize that lying is his most effective strategy against us. In fact, lying is not just, what Satan does, but it is a fundamental part of who he is: He has always hated the truth, because there is no truth in him. When he lies, it is consistent with his character; for he is a liar and the father of lies (see **Jn. 8:44**).

Accordingly, to defeat the devil at his game, you must know the truth well enough that you are able to recognize his deceptions.

I once heard about a man who inspected money for the Federal Reserve to detect counterfeit bills. Instead of spending a lot of time learning about the various counterfeits, he said his main strategy was to know the genuine bills so well that the counterfeits would appear obvious. That should be the same approach we use in detecting the devil's lies. Knowing this truth, how should you respond to an attack by Satan on your health?

The Bible is full of promises concerning your right to healing and health as a believer, and it encourages you to, *"let God be found true, though every man be found a liar."* (**Rom. 3:4, NASB**) That means that we need to believe the promises of the Lord instead of Satan's "lying symptoms." Here are just a few of the Lord's great promises for your healing:

> *"I will restore health to you and heal you of your wounds."* (**Jer. 30: 17.**)

> *"Bless the Lord, O my soul, and forget not all His benefits… who heals all your diseases; who redeems your life from destruction."* (**Ps .103:2-4.**)

> *"He was wounded for our transgressions, He was bruised for our iniquities; the chastisement for our peace was upon Him, and by His stripes we are healed."* **Isa. 53:5**

> *"[He] Himself bore our sins in His own body on the tree, that we, having died to sins, might live for righteousness; by whose stripes you were healed."* (**1 Pet. 2:24.**)

> *"Beloved, I pray that you may prosper in all things and be in health, just as your soul prospers,"* (**3 Jn. 2.**)

If you are struggling with some kind of physical sickness today, I encourage you to meditate on these verses and speak them to the circumstances in your life. Besides, remember: God's Word has an answer, not just, for your healing, but for every problem, you will ever face. It is a powerful offensive weapon that you can use to gain victory!

Whenever you face a battle, you can find a scriptural promise to stand on, giving you authority over the enemy.

Speak the Word

We can be confident that God's Word will accomplish its intended purpose in our lives and our circumstances.

The Lord tells us in Isaiah:

> *"So shall My word be that goes forth from My mouth; it shall not return to Me void, but it shall accomplish what I please, and it shall prosper in the thing for which I sent it."* **Isa. 55:11**

Merely, to have its maximum impact, Scripture must be believed and spoken. Instead of merely treasuring the Word in our heart (see **Ps. 119:11**), we should be confessing it from our mouth, as Paul encourages us: *"'The word is near you, in your mouth and in your heart' (that is, the word of faith which we preach)"* (**Rom. 10:8**).

God not only has given us His written Word to believe, but He has also authorized us to speak it. Just as the centurion said to Jesus in Luke, *"Say the word, and my servant will be healed,"* (**Lk. 7:7**), you and I have been given the authority to boldly speak God's Word!

To this extent, what do you need from Jesus today? A healing? A financial miracle? A restored relationship? Deliverance from an addiction? First, let God speak His Word to you; then you must speak His Word to your circumstances! Your miracle will come.

Remember: The God you serve is the same One who spoke the worlds into existence and said, *"Let there be light"* (**Gen. 1:3; Heb. 11:3**). One word from Him can easily give us whatever breakthrough we need. His word is near you, in your mouth and in your heart…so speak that word!

3. Enforcing Dominion in Prayer

You have been given a tremendous inheritance, but you must recognize it and claim it. If someone were to die and gave you a bequest in their will, you will probably receive a call or letter from the attorney handling the estate. They will inform you that you have been left a bequest of some kind—a house, a piece of property, some money, or some personal items. It is something you have inherited. You have a legal right to it.

It is yours now. However, the attorney will also probably inform you that you need to act upon your inheritance. You may need to go to the attorney's office or the courthouse, and there will undoubtedly be papers for you to sign. The inheritance belongs to you, but you still need to claim what is yours. The same is true with God's promises, dominion, and the authority He has delegated to you.

When Jesus died, he passed along this authority to you and me. It belongs to us now, but we need to step out in faith and obedience to receive our inheritance.

If we truly believe God's promises, we will want to implement them through prayer. Even Jesus Himself—though He was the Son of God—recognized His need for regular times of prayer to the Father.

Look at this stunning evidence: Early morning prayer. *"Now in the morning, having risen a long while before daylight, He went out and departed to a solitary place; and there He prayed."* (**Mk. 1:35.**)

Prayer was such a priority to Jesus that he got started *"a long while before daylight."*

Is it not amazing how much importance Jesus placed on prayer as a key to unlocking His power and authority? The disciples noticed this, and they wisely asked Jesus, *"Lord, teach us to pray."* (**Lk. 11:1.**) We have no record of them asking Him how to preach, heal the sick, or cast out demons, but they recognized that prayer was the secret to all these other spiritual activities.

Perhaps you would say to me today, "Pastor Ron, I have tried praying for what I need, but it just does not seem to work." Well, Jesus anticipated your question. Whenever He urges us to pray, He also mentions the need for persistence: *"Jesus told his disciples a parable to show them that they should always pray and not give up."* (**Lk. 18:1, NIV**)

Do not give up! Your breakthrough will come, but you need to persevere in your prayers: *"Ask, and it will be given to you; seek, and you will find; knock, and it will be opened to you."* (**Lk. 11: 5-13.**)

Spiritual Warfare

We are in a spiritual battle! Unfortunately, most of the time people do not recognize it. They are just looking at things from a natural, human perspective. They factor God, the devil, and the complete supernatural realm right out of the equation.

The average person does not realize the spiritual battle taking place. God does not send bad things our way. It is not just happenstance or fate. There is a real enemy out there that we must learn to deal with.

Most people recognize that actions are important in the physical realm. You know that there are consequences for what you do.

If you are speeding while driving, you could get a ticket or cause a wreck. The ticket could cost money and put points on your license. The wreck could damage cars or even cost someone their life. When we talk negatively about someone, we can hurt their feelings or even loose demonic powers against them. There is much more to life than just this physical, natural, surface level.

Spiritual dynamics are constantly taking place. Whether or not the person you are speaking evil about ever knows it, you will be affected. Venting anger, frustration, resentment, or unforgiveness affects you whether it affects anyone else or not. I have ridden with people who are very vocal in traffic when someone cuts them off. They have told me, "That person does not know what I said. They did not hear me." It does not matter whether they ever hear you or not. If you get angry and bitter, you have just yielded yourself to Satan. Whether you recognize it or not, the devil is listening.

God has given us a huge authority. As born-again believers, Jesus has given us more authority than even Adam and Eve had. They had authority over this Earth. However, after Christ rose from the dead, He had authority in heaven, authority on Earth, and authority under the Earth—meaning the demonic realm and hell (see **Phil. 2:10**).

> *After Jesus resurrected, but before He ascended, He turned to His disciples and said: All power [authority, power of rule] is given unto me in heaven and in earth. Go ye therefore, and teach all nations, baptizing them in the name of the Father, and of the Son, and of the Holy Ghost: teaching them to observe all things whatsoever I have commanded you: and, lo, I am with you always, even unto the end of the world. Amen."* **Matt. 28:11-20**

Since therefore refers to "in light of what I have just said," Jesus was basically telling His followers, "The authority and power I have, I now give to you. Go, and continue doing My work, the work that I have begun."

The authority we have as believers in Christ today is superior to the authority Adam had. We have everything back that he lost, and much more. We now have authority over the demonic realm (see **Matt. 10:1, 7–8**).

Like it or not, there is a spiritual battle raging right now for your heart and mind. As you think in your heart is the way that you will be (see **Prov. 23:7**). Your thoughts become what you say and do, with your actions being the greatest expression of your authority. Therefore, you will be influenced, dominated, and held captive by your own thoughts.

If you want to tap into the deep things of the Spirit do not read, listen to, and sing the same things that carnal Christians do.

Chapter 23
HOW-TO WALK-IN MIRACLES

"Do not be conformed to this world, but be transformed by the renewing of your mind, that you may prove what is that good and acceptable and perfect will of God." **Rom. 12:2**

It is true that some storms are of our own making. Jonah proved that (see **Jon. 1-3**). Jonah ran from God, encountered a storm while on a ship, was thrown overboard, and wound up in the belly of a fish. Although, these disciples were smack dab in the center of God's will when the storm hit in the Gospel of Matthew (see **Matt. 14**).

I am saying all this to point out that you cannot look at circumstances to tell you whether you are in God's will. You need a word from God. You need an inner witness from the Holy Ghost that what you are doing is what God told you to do. If you do not have that, it will hinder you from seeing His power manifest in your life. When problems come, you will feel condemned and think, "I brought this on myself; I deserve it."

You need to *know*, first, that you are doing what God told you to do.

Most of these disciples were fishermen on that very lake. I personally believe that the reason Jesus had to constrain them to get into the boat was that they knew that the conditions were ripe for a storm, and they did not want to be out on the water. If they had been thinking about the fact that Jesus had just fed 5,000 people, not including women and children (see **Matt. 14:15-21**), then they would have expected a miracle, because they were only out there at Jesus' direction. It was not their wisdom. They never would have done this if it were up to them. Even though, in the center of God's will is where you can hope to see the miraculous!

You see, Jesus was aware of their situation, and He was responsible for them being there. You might be in a situation right now where you are facing absolute disaster financially, physically, emotionally, or in your relationships. Maybe nothing seems to be working. If you are there because of your own rebellion and disobedience to God, then you need to do what Jonah did in the belly of the fish—repent (see **Jon. 2:1-9**). You need to say from your heart, "God, forgive me. I know I have been in rebellion toward You, but right now I make a change to follow You again." Get out of rebellion and get to where you are submitting to God. He loves you and wants to set you free.

So, are you a Peter or a Jonah? If you are amid a storm and you know that you are there because you have been following God, then you need to recognize that the Lord is responsible for you. Where He guides, He also provides. That is just a principle of God. Just as Jesus was aware of these disciples' plight, He is aware of your situation.

God is amid the storm with you. He cares for you more than you could possibly imagine. His power is present to set you free (see **Jn. 8:32**). Instead of expecting defeat, instead of meditating on tragedy, you need to expect a miracle from God. You have to get away from doing everything natural and only depending upon God as a last resort. God ought to be your first resort. God has miracles He wants to manifest in your life. The story of Peter walking on the water is power packed with truths. Walk on top of your problems instead of being overcome by them.

Getting Out of the Boat

Another powerful truth that is essential for the miraculous is that you must be willing to get out of the boat before you walk on water.

Most of the disciples were clinging to the slim hope that the boat gave them. They were in a raging storm, so it is probable that the boat was filled with water just like another time on that sea (see **Mk. 4:37**). It was foolish to step out of the boat onto the water, but that is what God told Peter to do. He had to go beyond his own ability and trust that God would keep him from sinking.

Likewise, many of us are afraid to step away from the world and out on the word that God has given us. We want the miraculous but do not want to leave the relative safety of what everyone else is doing. However, just like this boat, the world is in crisis. Without the Lord, it is going to sink. Why are we so afraid to leave the mundane and trust God for a miracle? Peter was willing to risk it all.

If you can live without the miraculous power of God, you will. Nevertheless, there should be something in you that is sick and tired of being sick and tired. God made each one of us for greatness, but not greatness by the world's definition; the Lord wants to release His miracle-working power in you. He wants to make your life better than your biggest dream.

There are reasons that some people see miracles and others do not. It is not fate or luck. It is not like lightning, where you never know when it will strike. God does not pick and choose; there are principles we must follow to see His power manifest. If you do not understand that, that is one of the reasons, you are having problems. By faith, you too, can see the miraculous power of God. (**Rom. 3:27**)

The instance where Peter walked on the water perfectly illustrates many of the truths that are essential to walking in the miraculous. This is recorded in the book of Matthew.

> *"And straightway Jesus constrained his disciples to get into a ship, and to go before him unto the other side, while he sent the multitudes away. And when he had sent the multitudes away, he went up into a mountain apart to pray: and when the evening was come, he was there alone. But the ship was*

now in the midst of the sea, tossed with waves: for the wind was contrary. And in the fourth watch of the night Jesus went unto them, walking on the sea. And when the disciples saw him walking on the sea, they were troubled, saying, It is a spirit; and they cried out for fear. But straightway Jesus spake unto them, saying, Be of good cheer; it is I; be not afraid. And Peter answered him and said, Lord, if it be thou, bid me come unto thee on the water. And he said, Come. And when Peter was come down out of the ship, he walked on the water, to go to Jesus." **Matt 14:22-29**

Notice in **verse 22** that the Lord had to constrain His disciples to get into the ship. The word *"constrained"* means to compel or urge. In other words, this is saying that there was resistance on the disciples' part to do what Jesus said. Despite, to their credit, they went ahead and submitted themselves to Him. They were doing exactly what Jesus told them to do. That is one of the essentials to receiving a miracle from God. Yet, look what **verse 24** says: *"But the ship was now in the midst of the sea, tossed with waves: for the wind was contrary."*

Some people have the mistaken belief that if they are really following God, then everything should be smooth sailing. That is how many people discern whether they are in the will of God. They look at their circumstances, and if everything is just perfect, then it must be God. Still, thinking you have missed God just because you have a problem is incorrect. This instance proves that. They were doing exactly what the Lord told them to do.

Believers Are Different

If you were arrested for being a Christian, would there be enough evidence to convict you? Sadly, most Christians do not have any noticeable differences in their lives when compared to an unsaved person. That is not the way it is supposed to be. Get out of the boat!

God intended for mankind to live in Him. As Acts says, *"In him we live, and move, and have our being."* (**Acts 17:28.**) He is supernatural. The things you see and experience here in this physical world do not limit him. The supernatural life is for you to be drawing upon God's ability and power. Let me put it this way: If you are not walking in the supernatural, miraculous power of God, you are living below your privileges, in a substandard life. That might seem strong, but it is true. If your life is not supernatural, then it is superficial. I really believe that.

Someone might say, "But Peter began to sink." That is true. Yet, Peter also walked on the water. That is something that only Jesus has ever done. Besides, when Peter began to sink, the Lord was right there to pick him up. He did not drown, and neither will you if you get out of the natural and begin to start walking in the supernatural.

Some of you might think, "Well, I do not need a miracle like this. I do not need to walk on water. What does this have to do with my situation?" Of course, I am not saying that God wants you to go physically walk on water. The significance of this is that here was a situation where it looked like the disciples might be killed and Peter was able to walk on top of what was trying to kill him.

What is trying to kill you? Is it sickness? How about financial problems or marital problems?—maybe it is just the mundane. Many people are suffering from boredom. Whatever it is, God wants to release His miracle-working power in you and put you on top. Nevertheless, it is up to you. It is His power that performs the miraculous, but Peter did not see that power in operation until he took a step outside of the boat.

The exact same principles that operated in Peter's life for him to walk on the water will work for you too!

How to Speak a Miracle

We have learned that as Jesus healed the sick, He *spoke* to the eyes, the lame man, to the leprosy, to the demons, to the fever (see **Lk. 4:39**). If we want to see manifestations of healing, we must imitate Jesus.

If you want to see a miracle, speak as Jesus did. Remember how Jesus spoke to Lazarus (who was dead). He said, Lazarus, *"Come forth!"* (see **John 11:43**.) This situation required a miracle not just healing!

You need these principles operating in your life to walk in the miraculous power of God.

BE BOLD to Declare:

* I will dominate temptation to sin, in Jesus' name.

* I will dominate feelings of anger.

* I will dominate feelings of revenge.

* I will dominate feelings of discouragement.

* I will honor the Lord for every good gift from heaven.

* I will dominate feelings of worry, doubt, and fear.

* I will dominate negative circumstances.

* I will live out of my spirit

In myself, I can do nothing. However, I am not just in myself (see Gal. 2:20 & Jn. 5:19).

Chapter 24
YOUR SUPER POWERFUL LIFE

> *"Then Peter said, "Silver and gold I do not have, but what I do have I give you: In the name of Jesus Christ of Nazareth, rise up and walk."* (**Acts 3:6**)

It was God's power that healed the crippled man in Acts, but that power was under Peter's authority (see **Acts 3:6**). Peter went on to say that it was faith in the name of Jesus that had wrought this miracle (see **Acts 3:16**). Although, Peter did not ask God to heal this man, he believed the Lord had already done His part and had placed that power within him. Now it was Peter's responsibility to release that power, and that is just what he did.

The Lord never told us to pray for the sick in the sense that we ask Him to heal them. He told us to heal the sick. There is a "big" difference between the two. It has to do with operating in the dominion and authority He has already given us. Look at the commands the Lord gave His disciples.

> *"then he called his twelve disciples together, and gave them power and authority over all devils, and to cure diseases. And he sent them to preach the kingdom of God, and to heal the sick."* **Lk. 9:1-2**

> *"And when he had called unto him his twelve disciples, he gave them power against unclean spirits, to cast them out, and to heal all manner of sickness and all manner of disease."* **Matt. 10:1**

> *"And as ye go, preach, saying, The kingdom of heaven is at hand. Heal the sick, cleanse the lepers, raise the dead, cast out devils: freely ye have received, freely give."* **Matt. 10:7-8**

It is God's Plan!

Jesus told us to heal the sick not pray for the sick. What a radical statement! This will get you kicked out of most churches today, but these are the exact words of our Lord Jesus. In addition, this is precisely why more people do not see the miraculous results they are praying for. They are not taking their authority and commanding the circumstances to bow to kingdom dominion; they are passively asking God to do what He told them to do.

I know this goes contrary to popular Christian doctrine. We are constantly told that it is not us but God who is the Healer, and I agree with that totally. Nevertheless, I also believe that God has placed His healing power under our authority, and it is up to us to release it. If we do not take our authority and become commanders instead of beggars, God's power will not be released. There needs to be a radical renewal of our thinking on this issue.

Peter had people line the streets so that if only his shadow would touch them, they would be healed (see **Acts 5:15**).

Look at an amazing passage of Scripture in Isaiah, *"Ask Me of things to come concerning My sons; And concerning the work of My hands, you command Me."* (**Isa. 45:11**.) What a powerful scripture! What does the Lord mean when He tells us to command Him? Well, He certainly does not mean we are mightier and more powerful than He is and can order Him around. He means, concerning the things He has already done, He wants us to take our authority and command His power.

God Given Authority

Most people think that God made Satan, but that is not so. God created Lucifer, a wonderful, powerful, godly angel, but it was mankind who made Satan. There is a difference between creating and making. This could revolutionize your whole approach toward the devil. Satan is not using some superhuman, angelic authority against us; he is using the authority and power that was given to man by God. Therefore, Satan cannot do anything to us without our consent and cooperation!

The only power that Satan has is the power of deception, and the worst thing about deception is that you do not know you are being deceived. Otherwise, it would not be deception. Once the truth is received, deception loses all its power. Therefore, Satan loses all his power when we know the truth.

Many people do not know the truth about Satan's defeat. In fact, many Christians are the very instrument the devil is using to foster the deception that he is still a powerful foe. (**1 Jn. 3:8**)

Your Enemy Has Been Conquered

We need to believe that Satan has already been destroyed; (see **Heb. 2:14**), and boldly "enforce" his defeat. The only power he has is the power to deceive. Our battle should be against the "wiles" (trickery) of the devil (see **Eph. 6:11**), not the devil himself. Any other approach is giving the devil authority and power, which he does not have, and he uses that to intimidate us. The only weapon Satan has is the power we give him when we believe his lies.

Warfare only takes place between two undefeated foes. Once an enemy has been conquered, the war is over. Satan is a defeated foe.

Colossians says, *"And having spoiled principalities and powers, he made a shew of them openly, triumphing over them in it,"* (**Col. 2:15, KJV**) The archaic meaning of the word "spoiled" here is "to plunder; despoil" (American Heritage Dictionary). This means that after Jesus defeated Satan, He stripped him of everything he had, specifically the keys of death and hell (see **Rev. 1:18**). Satan has no power to imprison anyone.

The Greek word that was translated "shew" in this verse (see **Col. 2:15.**) is *"deigmatizo"* which means "to exhibit" (Strong). This comes from the root word *"deigma"* which means "a specimen." Satan is like one of those bugs we had to capture for biology class. We caught it and then nailed it on a board with a little pin to exhibit for a class project. You need to picture the devil nailed like a bug on display. Praise the Lord!

You Are in Christ Now!

Your *super-powerful life* will begin when you get a *revelation* of the kind of power that resides in you through Christ Jesus.

Colossians is the place to get that *revelation*: *"For in Him (Christ) dwells all the fullness of the Godhead bodily. And you are complete in Him, which is the head of all principality and power."* (**Col. 2:9-10.**)

Wow! Let us meditate on this truth. After all that Jesus endured and accomplished in His life, death, resurrection, and ascension, God gave Him the highest name of authority in the universe (see **Phil. 2:6-11**).

Notice the scripture says that Jesus is *"head of all principality and power."* (**Col 2:10.**) The Greek word for *"principality"* is *arche*, meaning "rule" and "magistracy." The Greek word for *"power"* is *exousia*, which means "authority," or dominion. These two words, *principality and power,* used together, declare that Jesus has rulership over every government and kingdom in the universe.

The scripture also declares that we are *"complete in Him."* (**Col 2:10.**) The Greek word for *"complete"* is *pleroo*, which can mean, "to make full," "to fill up," "to cause to abound," "to fill to the top: so that nothing shall be wanting to full measure." We are members of God's kingdom, and

God (Father, Son, and Holy Spirit) is at work within us to produce what He desires.

We have inherited a victorious nature from our heavenly Father, though our Lord Jesus. Always remember that you are complete in Christ (see **Phil 1:6** and **Col 2:9-10**)!

Daily Applying Your Dominion

(according to **Romans 4:17** and **Mark 11:23**)
*Add your *voice of faith* to any medicine or procedure.

Mind oppression

Mind: I call you restored.
Mind: I call you healed and whole.
Cause of the problem: be dead at the root, according to **Mark 11:12-14**.
Spirit of confusion & destruction: I cast you out in Jesus' mighty name.

Cancer of the blood

Blood: I call you restored.
Blood: I call you healed.
Blood: I call you brand new & whole.
Cancer: be dead at the root, according to **Mark 11:12-14**.
Spirit of cancer: I cast you out – in Jesus' mighty name.

Cancer of anything (heart, kidney, lung, breast, prostate, etc.)

Body part: I call you restored.
Body part: I call you healed.
Body part: I call you brand new & whole.
Cancer: be dead at the root, according to **Mark 11:12-14**.
Spirit of cancer: I cast you out – in Jesus' mighty name.

Anything broken, missing, strained, or not working right

Body part: I call you restored.
Body part: I call you healed.
Body part: I call you brand new & whole.
Cause of the problem: be dead at the root, according to **Mark 11:12-14.**
Spirit of affliction: I cast you out – in Jesus' mighty name.
Bones, muscles, joints, ligaments: I call you healed, whole, and strengthened.

Dominion has a voice. Your mountain MUST hear your voice.

Printed in the USA
CPSIA information can be obtained
at www.ICGtesting.com
JSHW010805261124
74314JS00003B/4